Alamo Anthology

Other Eakin Press Books by William R. Chemerka

The Alamo Almanac And Book of Lists (1997)

This volume's title says it all! The book features three main sections: an introduction to the Texas Revolution and the Siege and Battle of The Alamo; an alphabetical section that contains numerous historical and popular culture entries, from Alamo defender Juan Abamillo to ZZ Top, the Texas-based rock band; and a diversified Lists section that features such rosters as "Alamo Couriers," "Top 20 Most Frequently Asked Questions at the Alamo," "15 Historical Descriptions of the Alamo" and the "Best" and "Worst" Alamo Movies, among many others.

The Alamo Almanac And Book of Lists also includes a select bibliography plus illustrations, photos and battle maps.

The Davy Crockett Almanac And Book of Lists (2000)

A followup of sorts to *The Alamo Almanac And Book of Lists*, this book chronicles everything one would want to know about the Alamo's most famous defender.

The book's first part focuses on the Crockett of history and features an overview of the famous frontiersman's life, excerpts from his 1834 autobiography, a "Crockett Family Tree" and a comprehensive time line. The other major section of this book features the remarkable story of Crockett as a symbol of popular culture over the centuries.

The Davy Crockett Almanac And Book of Lists also includes a select bibliography, photos, illustrations and maps of Crockett's homes.

Alamo Anthology

From the Pages of *The Alamo Journal*

Edited by

William R. Chemerka

EAKIN PRESS Fort Worth, Texas

*This book is dedicated to
my goddaughter, Megan Matera,
and my godson, David Vicaro.*

ALL RIGHTS RESERVED. No part of this book may be reproduced in any form without written permission from the publisher, except for brief passages included in a review appearing in a newspaper or magazine.

Copyright © 2005
By William R. Chermerka
Published By Eakin Press
An Imprint of Wild Horse Media Group
P.O. Box 331779
Fort Worth, Texas 76163
1-817-344-7036
www.EakinPress.com
ALL RIGHTS RESERVED
1 2 3 4 5 6 7 8 9
ISBN-10: 1-57168-669-X
ISBN-13: 978-1-57168-669-5
Library of Congress Control Number 2005930861

Contents

Preface	v
Acknowledgments	ix
Remembering Ed Eakin	x
The Alamo Society	xi
Introduction: Remember the Alamo! by William R. Chemerka	1
A Volley From the Darkness: Sources Regarding the Death of William Barret Travis by Stephen L. Hardin	17
Courage Under Fire: The Mexican Army at the Battle of the Alamo by William R. Chemerka	31
Where Did the 1824 Flag Fly? by Bill Walraven	41
James Butler Bonham: Oct. 17, 1835–March 6, 1836 by Thomas Ricks Lindley	47
Manning the Walls by Robert L. Durham	65
The Assault of the Alamo: An Evaluation of Santa Anna According to the Principles of War by William R. Chemerka	77
Archeological Evidence for the Defenses of the Alamo by James E. Ivey	89
Where Did Davy Die? by Robert L. Durham	105
Davy Crockett: A Hero for all Decades by William R. Chemerka	113

Latest from Texas 127
by Robert L. Durham

A Fortnight with James Bowie 137
edited by William C. Davis

Select Bibliography............................... 155

Preface

The Battle of the Alamo on March 6, 1836, was a remarkable event of the Texas Revolution, 1835-1836. As a matter of fact, it is one of the most memorable episodes in American history. It is a tale of bravery, sacrifice, courage, boldness, and valor.

In an old Spanish mission complex in San Antonio de Bexar, a small outnumbered Texian garrison, under the command of Lt. Col. William Barret Travis, fought to the death against a large Mexican army led by Gen. Antonio Lopez de Santa Anna. After the predawn battle ended, the bodies of the slain Alamo defenders—Davy Crockett, James Bowie, James Butler Bonham, Toribio Losoya, Almeron Dickinson, Robert Cochran, Richard Stockton and over 180 others—were burned and their remains scattered. Santa Anna called the battle "a small affair."

On April 21, 1836, at the Battle of San Jacinto, Gen. Sam Houston led his Texian army to victory against Santa Anna. During the battle, some of the Texians called out "Remember the Alamo!"—a rallying cry that would resonate in the hearts of many freedom-loving people for centuries to come.

America did indeed remember the Alamo.

In the decades that followed, a number of factors promoted and enhanced the reputation of those who fought during Texas' thirteen days of glory. Books, newspaper and magazine articles, poems, music, paintings, sculptures, plays, living history reenactments, and films embellished the Alamo's roll call of heroes.

In 1891, the Daughters of the Republic of Texas (DRT) was formed "to perpetuate the memory and spirit of the men and women who have achieved and maintained the independence of

Texas." The group's dedicated members act as the official custodians of the Alamo and its sacred grounds in downtown San Antonio, Texas. To be sure, the DRT has helped millions of visitors each year "remember the Alamo!"

The Texas Sesquicentennial in 1986 signaled an increase in creative works devoted to the Alamo. That same year marked the bicentennial of Davy Crockett's birth. Since that time more than a dozen Alamo books have been written, most being informative general histories. However, some students of the Alamo story have wanted to explore more about the Texas Revolution's most memorable military event.

In 1986, *The Alamo Journal*, the official publication of The Alamo Society, began to meet the demand for those who wanted to know more about the Alamo of history and the Alamo of popular culture. Over the years, a number of articles, penned by professional and amateur historians, have added to our collective understanding of the siege and battle of the Alamo. As a result of the contributors' efforts since the Texas Sesquicentennial, every major book written about the Alamo and its participants has included references from *The Alamo Journal*.

This humble volume features a representative sample of articles printed in *The Alamo Journal*.

Dr. Stephen L. Hardin examines the death of the Alamo commander in "A Volley From the Darkness: Sources Regarding the Death of William Barret Travis." The Alamo commander may have been one of the first defenders to fall in the predawn assault. However, accounts of his death varied in the nineteenth century and presented problems to historians a century later. Dr. Hardin's article originally appeared in *The Alamo Journal*, no. 59 (December 1987).

James E. Ivey furnishes the informative "Archeological Evidence for the Defenses of the Alamo." Since most of what was the physical Alamo has long since disappeared, historians have had difficulty recreating the image of what the mission–fortress exactly looked like during the memorable 1836 siege and battle. Ivey presents evidence that provides a more clear picture of the Alamo, particularly its exterior defense positions. Ivey's article originally appeared in *The Alamo Journal*, no. 117 (June 2000).

Thomas Ricks Lindley provides a vivid depiction of Alamo

defender "James Butler Bonham: October 17, 1835–March 6, 1836." Lindley goes beyond the telling of Bonham's familiar tale as the courier who returned to the Alamo. Evidence uncovered by Lindley and presented in this article casts an entirely different picture on how the Alamo garrison viewed its hopes for martial relief. The article originally appeared in *The Alamo Journal*, no. 62 (August 1988).

Much has been written about how Davy Crockett died, but Robert L. Durham investigates accounts that described the location of the famous Alamo defender's death in "Where Did Davy Die?" His article originally appeared in *The Alamo Journal*, no. 104 (March 1997).

Durham also explains the defense of the Alamo in "Manning the Walls." The Alamo was a huge complex and its defenders were few in number. The author said that the purpose of the article was "to provide a starting point to begin discussions that might lead to a greater understanding" of the Alamo's defenses. Durham assesses Alamo commander William B. Travis' dilemma in the article, which originally appeared in *The Alamo Journal*, no. 102 (Sept. 1996). He also contributes "Latest from Texas," an essay that appeared in issue no. 136 (March 2005).

William C. Davis provides an interesting analysis of a contemporary James Bowie account in "A Fortnight with James Bowie by the Rev. Benjamin Chase," which appeared in issue no. 126 (2002).

Bill Walraven explores the topic of Alamo banners in "Where Did the 1824 Flag Fly?" The tricolored standard with the year 1824 is the flag most closely associated with the Alamo, but Walraven explains that it probably didn't fly above the Alamo during the famous siege and battle. The article originally appeared in *The Alamo Journal*, no. 77 (June/July 1991) and was later reprinted in the author's book *The Magnificent Barbarians: Little-Told Tales of the Texas Revolution*.

This writer contributed "Courage Under Fire: The Mexican Army at the Battle of the Alamo," which originally appeared in *The Alamo Journal*, no. 67 (August 1989) and "The Assault of the Alamo: An Evaluation of Santa Anna According to the Principles of War," originally printed in *The Alamo Journal*, no. 80 (February 1992).

Besides the two aforementioned Alamo Journal articles, this writer penned "Remember the Alamo!" to serve as an introduction to the Texas Revolution, and "Davy Crockett: A Hero For All Decades," an address originally delivered on C-SPAN's Book TV in 2000.

Each of the essays that follow deals with a specific topic of Alamo history. Hopefully, these essays will raise more questions and inspire others to continue the historical investigation of the siege and battle of the Alamo.

Remember the Alamo!

WILLIAM R. CHEMERKA
June 2005

Acknowledgments

First and foremost, the authors who wrote the original articles which appeared in *The Alamo Journal* must be thanked for their cooperation: Texas' Dr. Stephen L. Hardin, Ohio's Robert L. Durham, Texas' Bill Walraven, New Mexico's James E. Ivey, Virginia's William C. Davis, and Texas' Thomas Ricks Lindley. Each of the authors is an expert in his own right on one or more aspects of the Alamo and the Texas War for Independence.

Thanks also to those artists who designed and illustrated the covers of *The Alamo Journal* which are reproduced in this book: New York's Gary Zaboly, New Jersey's Howard Bender and Washington's John Bourdage. Over the years, each of these artists has provided visual material which has embellished many an essay in the official publication of The Alamo Society.

Technical support was provided by James Sanderson, Keith Willoughby, Bryan Wilson and Patrick Colleton.

Additional thanks to Fess Parker, Don Vicaro, Gary Foreman, Ray Herbeck, Jr., Bill Groneman and his wife, Kelly, and the members of The Alamo Society.

My gratitude to the staff at Eakin Press for all of their creative efforts and support over the years.

As always, thanks to my wife, Deborah, for her assistance and encouragement.

Remember the Alamo!

Remembering
Ed Eakin

Eakin Press publisher, Ed Eakin, died prior to the publication of *Alamo Anthology*. He had printed hundreds of volumes, including two of my previous efforts: *The Alamo Almanac & Book of Lists* and *The Davy Crockett Almanac & Book of Lists*. As a matter of fact, *The Alamo Almanac & Book of Lists* was my first book.

I was familiar with Ed's books years earlier. What student of the Texas Revolution wasn't? He published books on the Alamo, the Gonzales 32, William B. Travis, Davy Crockett, James B. Bonham, Juan Seguin, James Bowie, Gregorio Esparza, Sam Houston, and San Jacinto, among others.

I first met him at a meeting of the Texas State Historical Association more than a decade ago and shared with him an idea for a book that ultimately became *The Alamo Almanac & Book of Lists*.

When he discovered that I was going to participate in the Texas Book Festival 2000, following the publication of *The Davy Crockett Almanac & Book of Lists*, he generously offered to let me stay with him and his wife, Charlene (and his old cat, "Miss Ethel"), at his home in Austin. Ed even picked me up at the airport, treated me to dinner, and drove me to the book festival! Was it Texas hospitality or Eakin hospitality? In any event, he certainly provided a personal touch to his authors. As one newspaper writer appropriately noted following his passing: He was "a tireless and committed publisher." That he was.

Thank you, Ed Eakin. Thanks for everything.

The Alamo Society

The Alamo Society is an international organization whose members are interested in one or more aspects of the Alamo, the Shrine of Texas Liberty. Our logo (above) reflects the diverse interests of the membership—from the Alamo of history (left) to the Alamo of popular culture (John Wayne's Alamo movie church appears on the right).

The official publication of The Alamo Society is *The Alamo Journal*, a magazine-like newsletter of research, news and opinion, which is published quarterly (March, June, September, and December).

Since the Texas Sesquicentennial in 1986, The Alamo Society has held an annual symposium. This yearly gathering has featured historians, writers, actors, painters, archeologists, living history participants, researchers, collectors—anyone with an interesting view of Texas' thirteen days of glory. Of course, Alamo Society members from around the world have also attended the annual symposiums, some from as far away as Australia!

The Alamo Society welcomes all who wish to "Remember the Alamo!"

Alamo Society Symposium Sites

1986	San Antonio, Texas
1987	Cincinnati, Ohio
1988	San Antonio, Texas
1989	San Antonio, Texas
1990	New York City, New York
1991	New York City, New York
1992	San Antonio, Texas
1993	San Antonio, Texas
1994	San Antonio, Texas
1995	San Antonio, Texas

1996	New Haven, Connecticut
1997	San Antonio, Texas
1998	San Antonio, Texas
1999	San Antonio, Texas
2000	San Antonio, Texas
2001	San Antonio, Texas
2002	Austin, Texas
2003	San Antonio, Texas
2004	San Antonio, Texas
2005	New York City, New York
2006	San Antonio, Texas

Anyone interested in joining The Alamo Society can contact the organization through its website: www:thealamosociety.com.

Introduction: Remember the Alamo!

"Remember the Alamo!"
Sam Houston
San Jacinto, 1836

The first quarter of the nineteenth century was a period of revolution in the Americas. Haiti, Venezuela, Argentina and Chile were but a few of Spain's colonies in the Western Hemisphere that had achieved independence in the century's first two decades. Like the United States in the late eighteenth century, these rebellious states sought freedom from oppressive foreign colonialism.

The Spanish empire, which at one time claimed nearly half of the so-called New World in the late fifteenth century, struggled to maintain its holdings in the Americas during the early nineteenth century. The powerful European nation originally came to the expansive lands across the Atlantic Ocean to exploit its precious metals and convert the native population to Christianity.

Spanish claims to what is now the southwestern United States were based upon the exploratory expeditions of Hernando DeSoto, Francisco Vasquez de Coronado, and other conquistadors. The Spanish built and developed forts, trading outposts, ranches, villages, and missions.

The missions were primarily established by Franciscan priests who attempted to Christianize the locals and teach them fundamental agricultural skills and other domestic crafts. Spain believed that such educational and religious programs at the missions would bind the native groups to the government for generations to come. The church, of course, was the center of all mission life. Built of adobe and stone, these missions included housing for the priests and instructional workshops that offered everything from blacksmithing and woodworking to jewelry-making and weaving. Usually, the entire mission complex was enclosed within adobe walls. The land surrounding the missions was cultivated for crops, especially corn. Herds of cattle and horses usually completed the look of a successful large-scale mission.

One such church complex was Mission San Antonio de Valero, which was completed around 1757. A mounted military unit, the Second Flying Company of San José y Santiago del Alamo de Parras, was later billeted at the mission and essentially gave the place its more common name: The Alamo.

Spanish colonial policy, however, was not based upon benevolence. Ruthless suppression, backed by soldiers, was usually the primary method of indoctrination for the local population. In time, revolts sprang up across Spain's American empire.

In 1821, Mexico broke free of the Spanish yoke. Three years later it created its own republican constitution modeled after the United States' document. Mexico—which included what is now Texas—sat at the southwestern border of the United States. Due to its geographic location, Mexico realized it could exploit the United States' expansionism for its own commercial gains. At that time, Texas was a land of economic opportunity, but it lacked abundant capital, a skilled work force and, most importantly, an entrepreneurial class. To promote that opportunity and help develop Texas further, Mexico offered liberal land grants to those from the United States who would settle in the lands west of the Sabine River.

As early as 1821, American families had settled in Spanish Texas under authority granted to Stephen F. Austin, whose father, Moses, had initially requested a colonial grant from the Spanish authorities a year earlier. Austin was not content to be the intermediary between land-hungry Americans and the Mexican government. The personal empressario became thoroughly involved in governmental affairs, serving on various groups and delegations. Austin even became a member of the Coahuila-Texas legislative branch. All of his energies, however, were focused on developing an American presence in Mexico. In time, American families crossed the Sabine River, the southwestern boundary of the United States at Louisiana, and entered Mexico. These first enterprising Anglo families numbered in the hundreds; Mexico wanted thousands. And it got them.

As an incentive, Mexico offered 177 acres of land to farmers and 4,428 acres to ranchers. As an added financial bonus, Mexico stated that no central taxes would be levied for six years to its new citizens from the east. But the government in Mexico City identified several restrictions that accompanied the generous land grants: Anglo immigrants would have to swear allegiance to Mexico, convert to Roman Catholicism, and pledge not to use slave labor. The restrictions may have seemed strict to some, but most newcomers did not mind. In fact, for several years Mexico did not vigorously enforce the restrictions. As a result of this policy of salutary neglect, Americans arrived by the thousands—and some brought their slaves. Nevertheless, they brought with them their agricultural, ranching, business, and entrepreneurial skills. But they also brought with them such American characteristics as representative democracy, private property, the profit motive, freedom of enterprise, and the "peculiar institution"—slavery.

By the end of the 1820s, the few thousand or so Mexicans in Texas were outnumbered nearly seven to one by the growing Anglo population. As a matter of fact, the number of slaves in Texas nearly equaled the native Mexican population. Texas was indeed rapidly developing, but not in the way that the Mexican government had originally planned.

The Mexican government, however, was quick to act. Legislation passed on April 6, 1830, restricted further colonization from the United States. In addition, the new laws forbade the importation of slaves, and levied taxes. Furthermore, the regional governments of Texas and its neighbor, Coahuila, were combined to promote administrative efficiency. Activists among the Anglos, the so-called Texians, initiated a revolt to separate themselves from Coahuila. Random armed skirmishes between Texian settlers and Mexican soldiers broke out in places like Anahuac and Velasco. Even Stephen F. Austin was imprisoned in

Mexico City in 1833 after he pleaded for an independent Texas—one independent from Coahuila.

Tennessean Sam Houston, who arrived in Texas at this time to conduct peace talks with the Commanches for President Andrew Jackson, placed the local squabbling within a larger framework. Writing to the chief executive in Washington D.C., Houston observed: "The people of Texas are determined to form a State Government and separate from Coahuila, and unless Mexico is soon restored to order and the Constitution revived and re-enacted, the Province of Texas will remain separate from the Confederacy of Mexico. If Texas is desirable to the United States, it is now in the most favorable attitude perhaps that it can be to obtain it on fair terms."

The conflicts of the early 1830s gave way to a revolutionary movement fueled, in part, by the dictatorship of Mexican General Antonio Lopez de Santa Anna, who forcefully suppressed a democratic revolt in Zacatecas in 1834. Santa Anna vowed to curb all challenges to his Centralist authority.

In the United States, patriotic American newspapers zealously echoed Houston's earlier sentiments. Noted the Philadelphia *Courier* about a New York City pro-Texas rally: "Texas, Texas. Crowded meetings and gun-powder speeches, calling down vengeance upon the oppressors of the Texonians, is the order of the day." Private funds were immediately raised for the liberty-threatened Texians and volunteers from the United States headed west.

President Jackson remained diplomatically neutral. In November 1835, he subsequently ordered Secretary of State John Forsyth to alert his district attorneys to curb intervention by individual Americans in Mexico's domestic problems. But the former hero of the Battle of New Orleans was sympathetic to Texian concerns; as a matter of fact, Jackson welcomed any independent actions that could manifest themselves into a free Texas. Texian aspirations, however, were not as uniform as readers of the Eastern press may have believed. The Texian revolutionaries, like their American counterparts in 1775, were divided. One faction of dissidents wanted a guarantee that its rights as Mexican citizens under the liberal Mexican Constitution of 1824 would be restored. Others, however, wanted a complete break from Santa Anna's dictatorship—an independent nation, the republic of Texas.

In any event, revolutionary forces began to mobilize. From October 15 until November 1, 1835, the rebel government was the San Felipe-based General Council, headed by president R. R. Royall. The ad hoc council formed volunteer ranging companies of citizen–soldiers, sought financial aid from U.S. citizens and encouraged privateers to attack Mexican ships in the Gulf of Mexico, among other venturesome efforts. In time, the General Council yielded to the more formal Consultation, whose delegates elected Dr. Branch T. Archer of Brazoria as president. The delegates, who hailed from a dozen Texian districts, opted at first for a separation from Coahuila and a restoration of rights. Independence from Mexico was not a majority opinion. At least not yet.

However, some delegates quickly abandoned hope of reconciliation. Mina delegate D. C. Barrett called Santa Anna the "Usurper," a term similar to one Thomas Jefferson had used in the Declaration of Independence to describe Great Britain's King George III. Noted Barrett: "We declare and resolve that we are ... at war with Santa Anna and his supporters...."

By mid-November, the delegates selected Stephen F. Austin as a commissioner to the United States. Henry Smith was elected governor and Sam Houston was appointed commander of the embryonic regular army. Although the revolutionary government was finally organized, the first shots of the Texas Revolution had actually been fired a month earlier at Gonzales. The incident occurred when a mounted Mexican unit commanded by Lt. Francisco Castañeda was thwarted in its attempt to retrieve an artillery piece from an armed group of Texians that defiantly challenged the attackers to "Come and Take it."

Texas was alive with military activity. Volunteers arrived at Gonzales with little more than a flintlock weapon, one suit of clothes and a bedroll. Without martial organization, a supply system or a medical corps, the Texians initially substituted enthusiasm for material substance. In time, Austin was elected as military commander.

At the time, Castañeda and all other Mexican units in Texas were under the command of General Martin Perfecto de Cos who had been based in San Antonio since September with over 1,000 men and nearly two dozen pieces of artillery. Cos was entrusted by Santa Anna to curb the growing rebellion by capturing the rebel leaders and disarming the others. However, the armed Texians had plans of their own.

In the early morning hours of October 10, 1835, a Texian company under the command of Captain George M. Collinsworth skirmished with a small Mexican detachment at Goliad and captured the fortress. Presidio La Bahia became the Texian's strongest military base.

Military operations were initiated at additional locations. On October 28, a force of nearly 100 Texians under the command of James Bowie defeated a larger Mexican unit at Mission Concepcion outside of San Antonio.

At San Felipe, a convention was organized to discuss the status of the revolutionary state of Texas. Some delegates immediately argued for independence. Houston, on the other hand, stated that if independence was declared the moderate Mexicans, the so-called liberals, would abandon their sympathies for the Texians and support Santa Anna. Support for the Mexican Constitution of 1824 was declared—not independence from Mexico—and Houston was named commander of all Texians in the field; Edward Burleson was named commander of Texian troops at San Antonio de Bexar. Henry Smith was named governor and a legislature of sorts was created. Austin, the most respected of all the Texians, gave up his military leadership role and became a representative of the rebellious state to the United States.

The Texas Revolution was not only fought on land; as a matter of fact, the struggle featured a number of heated contests in the Gulf of Mexico. The first naval conflict occurred on September 1, 1835, when the Texian steamer *Laura* engaged in a skirmish of sorts with a Mexican ship, *Correo de Mejico*. The *Laura* possessed no naval guns, but its deck served as a firing position for its armed militia. The General Council initiated resolutions to create a navy, but like the United States in 1776, this embryonic fleet was more or less a flotilla of privateers. Captains of these vessels sought to capture Mexican craft as prizes rather than coordinate plans of operation with Texian land forces. In time, however, ships such as *Independence*, a ten-gun schooner, engaged in operations as far south as Tampico, Mexico.

Texian-initiated military operations continued into the autumn. In early November several dozen Texians under Ira J. Westover captured the earthen fortification known as Fort Lipantitlan, and later curbed an attack by a Mexican force nearly twice their size on the Nueces River. The control of Fort Lipantitlan by the Texians reduced General Cos' ability to be properly supplied in his San Antonio de Bexar headquarters.

Despite these initial victories, not all Texian military operations on land were successful during late 1835. An attempt to capture the Mexican port of Tampico in November was a complete failure. The small attacking force was captured and sentenced to death. One of President Andrew Jackson's diplomats in Mexico City, George R. Robertson, attempted to purchase the freedom of the twenty-seven condemned men but was rejected by Santa Anna's government. On December 14, all of the captured men, some of whom were Europeans, were shot to death.

Less than a week before the executions, the Texians scored their most important military success of the young rebellion. A force under General Edward Burleson stationed near San Antonio de Béxar attacked the Mexican settlement on December 5, 1835. The assault was initiated as a two-prong movement led by Colonels Francis W. "Frank" Johnson and Ben Milam. The fierce fighting took place over several days as Mexican and Texians battled from street to street and house to house before Cos capitulated on December 10. The Texians won control of the town and its nearby mission-fortress, the Alamo. But the victory was not without its costs. Some two dozen Texians were wounded in the Battle of Béxar; several were killed including the 47-year-old Milam.

Gen. Burleson's terms to Cos were without malice. He requested that the Mexican soldiers respect the Constitution of 1824, abandon Texas and pledge not to return. By December 25, Cos' army, sans artillery and some of its supplies, crossed the Rio Grande on its return to Mexico City. At year's end, Texas was free of Mexican soldiers. But the Texian victory was marred by departing volunteers who longed for home; in fact, some believed that for all practical purposes the revolution was over.

Others joined an ill-fated military scheme to capture Matamoros, Mexico under the command of Frank Johnson and James Grant. "The clothing sent here ... was taken from us by the arbitrary measures of Johnson and Grant, taken from men who endured all the hardships of winter ...," wrote Alamo commander Col. James Neill to Governor Smith and the Council on January 6, 1836. "I want here, for this garrison, at all times 200 men, and I think 300 men, until the repairs and improvement of fortifications are completed...." By January of 1836 the size of Texian forces in Béxar numbered just over 100 men.

Burleson's defeat of Cos in December was the catalyst which prompted Santa Anna, to invade rebellious Texas, reclaim San Antonio de Béxar and suppress the the remnants of the so-called revolution. Santa Anna, the self-proclaimed "Napoleon of the West," planned to personally lead the army. By late December, the Army of Operations, over 4,000 men strong, headed north. On January 20, 1836, Santa Anna ordered his second-in-command, General Vicente Filisola and General Ramirez y Sesma to "stop all communications with Bejar, without permitting the passage of food supplies, only allowing trustworthy and discerning spies to pass, who may be able to tell with certainty the conditions found in that city...."

The harsh winter of 1835-1836 further tested the resolve of the men under Neill's command at the Alamo. Meanwhile, Santa Anna's soldados marched onward through the snow-filled mountains. His army reached the Rio Grande on February 17, and was joined by another Mexican brigade, a force of some 1,500 men under command of General Ramirez y Sesma. Within a week, advance units of Sesma reached San Antonio de Béxar.

On February 23, 1836, the siege of the Alamo had begun. Sesma's soldiers raised a red flag atop the San Fernando church in the town, which signaled that the Alamo's defenders were to receive no quarter if captured. Shortly thereafter, Mexican artillery began a relentless pounding of the Alamo.

News of the Alamo siege quickly reached the United States. One Louisiana newspaper proclaimed: "Texas Forever! The usurper of the South has failed in his efforts to enslave the freemen of Texas. The wives and daughters of Texas will be saved from the brutality of Mexican soldiers. Now is the time to emigrate to the Garden of America." Of course, the newspaper statement was not purely patriotic; in fact, part of the statement was strictly economic: "A free passage, to all found, is offered at New Orleans to all applicants. Every settler receives a location of eight hundred acres of land."

Meanwhile, at the Alamo, few of its defenders were thinking of land. Mexican reinforcements arrived daily and artillery batteries began their destructive work.

The command structure at the Alamo had changed since Cos' capitulation. Col. James C. Neill, who commanded the gallant garrison, left for home on February 14 to attend to pressing family health problems. The command of the old Spanish mission was entrusted to Lt. Colonel William Barret Travis, a twenty-six-year-old South Carolinian, although sentiment among some of the volunteers sided with James Bowie, the forty-year-old Kentuckian who arrived at the Alamo with discretionary instructions from Gen. Sam Houston to destroy and abandon the Alamo. Some in the 150-man garrison, perhaps preferred David Crockett, the forty-nine-year-old former congressman who had arrived in Béxar only weeks earlier, to be commander. However, the famous frontiersman opted for the rank of "high private."

Crockett's arrival at the Alamo was memorable—and rightly so. Enrique Esparza recalled that "there was great cheering when Sénor Crockett came with his friends. He wore a buckskin suit and a coonskin cap. He made everybody laugh and forget their worries." On February 25, Alamo commander William Barret Travis wrote to Sam Houston and remarked: "The Hon. David Crockett was seen at all points, animating the men to do their duty." Crockett's popularity among the Texians was even echoed some ninety miles away at Goliad, where Captain John Sowers Brooks wrote his mother: "We have just received additional intelligence from Bexar. The Mexicans have made two successive attacks on the Alamo in both of which the gallant little garrison repulsed them with some loss. Probably Davy Crockett 'grinned' them off."

Travis, Bowie, Crockett and the other Alamo defenders were a diverse group. Several were Tejanos, like Juan Abamillo and

Toribio Losoya, who were Mexican born. Others hailed from such countries as Great Britain, Denmark and the German principalities. The majority, however, came from the United States. They made their way to Texas from Alabama, Pennsylvania, Massachusetts, Tennessee, Maine, New Jersey, Virginia, and over a dozen other states. Some had lived in Texas for several years, like George Washington Cottle of Missouri. Others, like William H. Fontleroy of Kentucky, had arrived only months earlier. In early 1836, however, they all considered themselves Texians.

To be sure, the Alamo had physically deteriorated since its secularization in 1793. Col. Neill and engineer Green Jameson fortified the old mission and strengthened some of its more glaring weak spots, namely the lengthy opening between the church and the South Wall. And the old adobe walls were augmented with twenty-one artillery pieces, making the Alamo one of the largest artillery parks in North America at the time. Guns ranging in size from two small brass pieces, and several workhorse three and four-pounders to an impressive 18-pounder, punctuated the walls and main courtyard. At least one artillery piece supported the palisade area. The roofless Alamo church's interior was transformed into an elongated dirt and stone gun ramp featuring a platform mounted at the building's elevated eastern side. Three guns protected the back of the old church.

Travis did not wait for the Mexicans to attack. He sent out numerous messengers with pleas for help. Travis' letter of February 24, 1836, is memorable for its determination, spirit and singularity of purpose.

> To the People of Texas and All Americans in the World—
> Fellow Citizens and Compatriots:
> I am besieged by a thousand or more of the Mexicans under Santa Anna. I have sustained a considerable Bombardment and cannonade for 24 hours and have not lost a man. The enemy has demanded surrender at discretion, otherwise the garrison is the be put to the sword, if the fort is taken. I have answered the demand with a cannon shot, and our flag still waves proudly from the walls. I shall never surrender or retreat. Then, I call on you in the name of Liberty, of patriotism, and everything dear to the American character, to come to our

aid with all dispatch. The enemy is receiving reinforcements daily and will no doubt increase to three or four thousand in four or five days. If this call is neglected I am determined to sustain myself as long as possible and die like a soldier who never forgets what is due his honor and that of his country.

Victory or Death!

Help did come. On March 1, 1836, a small relief force from Gonzales arrived, increasing the size of the garrison to over 200 defenders. However, the number of active combatants was reduced due to illness and disease. James Bowie was probably one of the more seriously ill men. Still, they held out. Perhaps Fannin would arrive with his force from Goliad, they thought. Perhaps Houston's army was not far off. What of other volunteer units? A letter dated March 1 from Maj. R. M. Williamson pledged more than 600 reinforcements. "For God's sake hold out until we can assist you," wrote Williamson.

On March 2, 1836, Texas formally declared itself an independent republic at a meeting of delegates to a general convention at Washington-on-the-Brazos. Word of the new Republic of Texas, however, never reached the Alamo. That same day, Texian Commander-in-Chief of the Army, Sam Houston issued a desperate broadside: "War is raging on the frontiers. Bejar is besieged by two thousand of the enemy, under command of general Sesma. Reinforcements are on the march, to unite with the besieging army. By last report, our force in Bejar was only one hundred and fifty men strong. The citizens of Texas must rally to the aid of our army, or it will perish."

Three days later, Santa Anna decided the siege of the Alamo had gone on long enough. On the afternoon of March 5, the general created his plan of attack for the next morning. His army would assault the Alamo in four columns, led by General Cos, Col. Francisco Duque, Col. Jose Maria Romero and Col. Juan Morales, respectively. In order to scale some of the Alamo's massive walls, several soldados were issued scaling ladders and tools, including crow bars.

Santa Anna's orders read: "The first column will be commanded by General Don Martin Perfecto Cos, and in his absence, by myself.

"The Permanent Battalion of Aldama (except the company

of grenadiers) and the three right centre companies of the Active Battalion of San Luis, will compose the first column.

"The second column will be commanded by Colonel Don Francisco Duque, and in his absence, by General Don Manuel Fernandez Castrillon: it will be composed of the Active Battalion of Toluca (except the company of Grenadiers) and the three remaining centre companies of the active Battalion of San Luis.

"The third column will be commanded by Colonel Jose Maria Romero, and in his absence, by Colonel Mariano Salas; it will be composed of the Permanent Battalions of Matamoros and Jimenes.

"The fourth column will be commanded by Colonel Juan Morales, and in his absence, by Colonel Jose Minon; it will be composed of the light companies of the Battalions of Matamoros and Jimenes, and of the Active Battalion Battalion of San Luis."

Santa Anna added that "the men will wear neither overcoats nor blankets, or anything that may impede the rapidity of their motions."

In the predawn darkness of March 6, 1836, nearly 2,000 Mexican infantryman, some shouting "Viva Santa Anna" as the buglers played the bloodcurdling *Deguello*, attacked the Alamo's walls. Despite the absence of sunlight, Alamo artillery and muzzleloading shoulder-arms fire generated enough firepower to alter the assault routes of the attacks. Without much hesitation, the Mexicans columns reformed and pressed the assault. Texian guns had forced an unplanned concentration of the Cos, Duque (Castrillon commanding following Duque's wounding) and Romero columns on the north wall. The Texians were also effective in shifting Morales' column away from the wooden palisade. Morales' men regrouped near the southwest corner of the compound at the base of the Alamo's 18-pound gun and charged again.

Musket and rifle fire filled the air with smoke as the Battle of the Alamo continued. Unable to scale the Alamo walls with the initial four-column assault, Santa Anna ordered the reserve troops under Colonel Agustin Amat into the battle. The respected Zapadores Battalion and five grenadier companies under Amat helped the struggling infantry to scale the North

Wall. Simultaneously, many of Cos' men broke through an opening along the northern portion of the West Wall. As a result of Mexican penetration, the Texians immediately abandoned the walls. In less than a half hour, the Mexican infantry had command of the Alamo's main courtyard.

The remains of the Texian defense was concentrated in the fortified rooms of the Long Barracks and the church. Perhaps a few isolated rooms along the South and West Walls also held handfuls of determined defenders, but their fate was sealed. A small number of Texians was isolated in the area immediately in front of the church. Mexican infantrymen turned Texian artillery about and fired into the wooden doors of the rooms. Each broken door was followed by an assault of soldados. Some of the bloodiest fighting of the battle took place in these darkened, smoke-filled rooms.

Finally, the battle claimed the lives of the last Texian effectives, possibly Crockett and several others, in the courtyard of the church. A few last stands took place in random, isolated rooms in the Long Barracks and inside the church. In these darkened chambers, combatants struggled to the death in hand-to-hand clashes.

A number of defenders attempted to escape from the defenses; however, they met their fate at the hands of Mexican cavalry stationed outside of the Alamo's walls. Second Lieutenant Manuel Loranca of the Dolores Cavalry regiment recalled that "Sixty-two Texians who sallied from the east side of the fort were received by the lancers and all killed."

When the fighting ended, probably 250 or more Texians lay dead. The publication *El Mosquito Mexicano* stated that 257 Texians had fallen during the Battle of the Alamo. And several hundred Mexican soldiers were either killed or wounded.

By the time the sun rose in the east, the Battle of the Alamo was over. After entering the Alamo, Santa Anna ordered the bodies of the Texian dead to be burned. A handful of women and children non-combatants, including the only Anglo woman, Susanna Dickinson, were allowed to leave unmolested. To Santa Anna, the events of March 6, 1836, were "but a small affair," but there were still other military objectives to accomplish. A larger Texian force at Goliad, a more formidable fortress under the command of James Fannin, had to be taken. In addition, Juan Seguin's rebel mounted unit had to be captured and other relief columns had to be countered. And Houston's army was still somewhere in the field.

Sam Houston arrived in Gonzales on March 11, and was informed that the Alamo had fallen. Initially refusing to publicly accept the news of the Alamo's fall so not to start a panic among the civilian population, the commander-in-chief officially acknowledged the tragedy two days later.

Fighting erupted between Mexican forces and Texian troops at Refugio. A small detachment of men from Goliad under the command of Captain Amon B. King had arrived on March 12 to help evacuate the locals from the approaching Mexicans, but the unit spent too much time harassing suspected supporters of San Anna's regime. A small unit of lancers from General Urrea's cavalry arrived and battled with King's men, but was later dispersed when reinforcements under the command of Colonel William Ward approached from Goliad. A large Mexican force arrived on the 14th and the Texians retreated to Mission Rosario where they temporarily held off several assaults. Outnumbered, the Texians fled during the night but a number of them were later captured and executed.

Temporary government officials were elected at Washington-on-the-Brazos on March 17, with New Jersey-born David G. Burnet assuming the role of president of the new republic; Lorenzo de Zavala was elected vice president. The new government soon abandoned the settlement since it was particularly vulnerable to Santa Anna's advancing forces.

On the same day, Houston and his force of several hundred volunteers reached Burnham's ferry on the Colorado River and anticipated word that Fannin's Goliad command would arrive to augment his ranks. Two days later, Houston retreated east to Beason's Crossing where additional volunteers poured in. Many of the latest armed men had heard of the Alamo's fall and were prepared to fight for Texas' independence.

Two weeks after the fall of the Alamo, Santa Anna's troops scored another victory. On March 20, Fannin surrendered near Coleto Creek to General Jose Urrea, who had previously defeated Texian forces at Agua Dulce, San Patricio and Refugio.

The Texians believed they would treated as prisoners of war who would eventually be sent to New Orleans. However, on March 27, Santa Anna ordered Urrea to carry out the execution of Fannin's Goliad command. Santa Anna stated: "The supreme government has ordered that all foreigners taken with arms in their hands, making war upon the nation, shall be treated as pirates." Nearly 400 men, save a handful of doctors, engineers and mechanics, were executed, although several dozen managed to escape by crossing the San Antonio River.

The Texian civilian population fled east, away from the advancing Mexicans.

On March 30, at Harrisburg, President David G. Burnet repeated Houston's earlier plea to the citizens of the new republic: "Your country demands your aid. The enemy is pressing upon us; families, the wives and children of your neighbors are driven from their firesides and compelled to take shelter in woods and forests, while the enemy gathers confidence and audacity from every disaster we encounter."

The following month, however, Santa Anna's string of victories came to an end. He was finally defeated at San Jacinto on April 21, 1836, as the cries "Remember the Alamo" and "Remember Goliad" were shouted by attacking Texian troops under Sam Houston's command. Santa Anna and over 4,000 of his soldiers were instructed to leave the Republic of Texas and return to Mexico. The Texas Revolution was over. Texas had won its independence.

"Travis' Vigil" by Gary Zaboly, Alamo Journal, no. 111 (December 1998)

A Volley from the Darkness: Sources Regarding the Death of William Barret Travis

by Stephen L. Hardin

Although his martyrdom at the Alamo made William Barret Travis a genuine American hero, his death is still shrouded in mystery. As befits a legendary figure, many stories concerning his last moments fall into the realm of folklore. Over the century and a half since the Battle of the Alamo, enduring myth and solid fact have become thoroughly intertwined, making careful analysis difficult, but at least four unanswered questions remain. Was Travis killed by enemy fire or by his own hand? What was Travis wearing on March 6, 1836? What were his last words? And finally, did Travis engage in a hand-to-hand death struggle with a Mexican general?

A good starting point is Walter Lord's *A Time to Stand* (1961), one of the few Alamo studies based firmly on primary materials. Lord wrote: "Travis sprang from his blanket ... seized his sword, double-barreled shotgun and homespun jacket of Texas jeans. Telling his slave Joe to follow, he ran across the plaza, leaped to the wall of the north battery. 'Come on boys,!' he shouted. The Mexicans are upon us and we'll give them Hell' ... No time to put on his coat, he slung it over a peg by a cannon and turned back to his troops. Spying a couple of [Juan N.] Seguin's company, he switched briefly to Spanish: '*No rendirse, muchachos* (Don't surrender, boys) ... a volley rang out from the darkness, Travis spun, hit in the head. His shotgun fell among the enemy; he himself within the fort, rolling down the bank of earth piled against the wall. He ended up sitting on the slope near a cannon, stunned and dying."[1]

Only Joe, the sole surviving Texian witness to Travis' death, knew the facts, and therein lies a major problem. By all reports the slave was intelligent and truthful, but apparently illiterate and therefore unable to leave his own written account. Of course, hundreds of soldados may have seen Travis fall but they were hardly to know him among the other defenders on the wall.

Although unable to write, Joe did talk and two Texians separately transcribed his account. Their versions matched, even to the point of the words and phrases he used. On March 20, fourteen days after the final assault, he told his sad tale to President David G. Burnet and his cabinet. William Fairfax Gray, a Virginia lawyer who was present, recorded Joe's statement: "Joe was sleeping in the room with his master when the alarm was given. Travis sprang up, seized his rifle and sword, and called to Joe to follow him. Joe took his gun and followed. Travis ran across the Alamo [plaza] and mounted the wall, and called out to his men, 'Come on boys, the Mexicans are upon us, and we'll give them hell.' He discharged his gun; so did Joe. In an instant Travis was shot down. He fell within the wall, on sloping ground, and sat up."[2]

George Campbell Childress, author of the Texas Declaration of Independence, must have also talked to Joe, for in a Tennessee newspaper interview he stated: "The servant of the lamented Travis says his master fell near the close of the siege [and that] on Sunday morning about three o'clock the guard upon the wall cried out, 'Col. Travis the Mexicans are coming!... Col. Travis sprang from his blanket with his sword and gun, mounted the rampart... discharged his double-barreled gun [and then]... he was immediately shot, his gun falling upon the enemy and himself within the fort."[3]

The primary evidence seems clear—Travis ran to the North Wall where he was struck down by enemy fire. Whether he was killed or merely stunned is unclear. But the issue became muddled when another version circulated that he had committed suicide. That story began when Bexar native Antonio Perez told vaqueros Andres Barcena and Anselmo Borgarra that Travis had stabbed himself rather than surrender. The two Tejanos repeated that account to General Sam Houston, who in turn passed it along in several letters.[4]

The story quickly took on a life of its own. Indeed, the same issue of the newspaper containing the Childress account also reported that "Col. Travis, the commandant, committed suicide as soon as he lost all hope."[5] In a 1931 dissertation, Amelia Williams bolstered the rumors when she misquoted Bexar alcalde Francisco Antonio Ruiz, claiming he wrote that the only wound on Travis was "a *pistol* [emphasis mine] shot through the forehead."[6] Although she did not say the wound was self-inflicted, the implication was obvious; a person would be far more apt to shoot himself with a pistol than a cumbersome long rifle or shotgun. Ruiz did in fact write that Travis was "shot *only* in the forehead," but that the bullet came from a pistol was pure fancy on Williams' part.[7]

The Travis suicide myth is easily refuted. People who could have known nothing firsthand began the story, and Williams based her impression on a misreading of the Ruiz account. But most importantly, Joe—who was standing beside Travis at the time—stated categorically that his master was hit by enemy fire. Joe never revealed in which part of his body Travis received the round, but Ruiz was specific on that point. That the ball should strike him in the head was in no way odd, since he was fighting behind a parapet with only the upper part of his body exposed.

A second controversy surrounds Travis' attire. Lord described a jacket made of "homespun Texas jeans" but that assertion is undoubtedly an assumption, not based on an eyewitness. The first reference to the jacket appeared in 1889, when the *San Antonio Express* published an interview with Mexican veteran Felix Nunez (later reprinted in the *Fort Worth Gazette*). Eighty-five years old at the time, he claimed to have participated in the battle fifty-three years earlier and that he "found Col. Travis' coat ... hanging on a peg driven [in]to the wall just behind the cannon from where his dead body had been dragged away."[8] Since Nunez's account is filled with errors, his claim that the coat belonged to Travis is far from reassuring. The old man remembered the siege lasting only four days; it continued for thirteen. He stated that the final assault came on Wednesday rather than Sunday; he claimed that Tejano defenders were permitted to leave; they, of course, died with their Anglo comrades. Further he confused the commanders of the assault columns.

Many of these errors may be attributed to an old man's faulty memory, but the other mistakes that run rampant through his narrative make his account even more dubious. Nunez "recalled distinctly" a fanciful story of a disguised Santa Anna attending a San Antonio fandango before the siege even began. "Here," he recalled, "the president completely disguised was talking and chatting in company with some Americans who had come over from the Alamo and participated in the festivities of the dance, not even dreaming that they were in such close proximity to one who would shortly spread before them the last and fatal feast of death."[9] Clearly, the anciano was not above "seasoning" his narrative with imaginary episodes. Santa Anna may have wished to be in Bexar on the night of the dance (February 22, 1836), but he was camped twenty-five miles below the city on the south bank of the flooded Medina River.[10] If Nunez fabricated the Santa Anna-as-secret-agent story, he might have invented the jacket tale. This is entirely possible, especially since he conveniently claimed to have burned the garment before anyone else could see it. There is, consequently, little in his account to recommend it for serious consideration.

Even if Nunez did pick up a jacket, there is no evidence that it belonged to Travis. Indeed, several factors argue against it. He could not have known Travis from any other Texian. By his own admission, he found the jacket "hanging on a peg," and could not have known who hung it there. In contradiction to José Enrique de la Peña and other more reliable Mexican participants, Nunez centered the battle in the Alamo church. He maintained the entire garrison "had taken refuge inside the church, and the front door of the main entrance fronting the west was open. [One can only speculate why a group of besieged men would take refuge inside a building and then fail to barricade the main entrance.] Just outside of this door Colonel Travis was working on a cannon."[11] According to other more reliable sources, Travis defended the North Wall.[12] If Nunez found a jacket where he indicated—near the front door of the shrine—

Travis could not have left it there. The old veteran mentioned papers inside the jacket but never established a link between them and Travis. Quite simply, no reliable primary evidence exists to support the contention that Travis died wearing a homespun jacket of Texas jeans.

Still, Walter Lord did dispel the myth, fostered by Alamo portraiture and popular illustration, that Travis wore a uniform.[13] But the fact remains that there is no way of knowing what Travis wore on the last day of the siege. Neither Joe, Francisco Ruiz, nor any of the Mexican participants ever said what he wore. But given the hectic nature of the siege, Travis undoubtedly slept that last night in trousers and shirtsleeves. And when the final assault began—as Joe suggested—Travis "sprang from his blanket" and ran straight from his cot to the North Wall, that is most likely what he was wearing when he was killed.

A third dispute concerns Travis' last words. Walter Lord as well as Travis biographer Professor Archie P. McDonald offered the traditional view. Both agreed that among Travis' final words were the Spanish admonition: *"No rendirse muchachos!"* In 1883, Irish Texan John Joseph Linn introduced this quotation in *Reminiscences of Fifty Years in Texas*. He obtained this information from "old Borgarra," or Alselmo Borgarra, who was involved in the Travis suicide rumors.[14] But here again Borgarra provided questionable information. He was in the Bexar area during the battle, but could not have been privy to many details. If, on March 6, he could have been inside the walls of the Alamo and within earshot of Travis he would have met the same fate as the other Tejanos found there. On the other hand, Gray had Joe saying that among his master's last words were: "Come on boys, the Mexicans are upon us and we'll give them Hell"—obviously a rallying cry. Travis may have shouted additional orders once he mounted the north battery but there is no primary evidence to support the notion that *"No rendirse, muchachos"* was among them. Like so many pieces of the Alamo puzzle, his last words are lost.

And lastly, of all the questions, perhaps the most intriguing is that of the alleged clash between Travis and Mexican General Mora. Gray's diary described the confrontation as follows: "As Travis sat wounded on the ground [after receiving the head shot]

General Mora, who was passing him, made a blow at him with his sword, which Travis struck up, and ran his assailant through the body, and both died on the spot. This was poor Travis' last effort."[15]

In turn, Childress, while not specifying Mora by name, wrote: "The Mexican general ... seeing the bleeding Travis, attempted to behead him; the dying Colonel raised his sword and *killed him!*"[16]

For many years afterward, writers incorporated this encounter in their works. As early as July 1836, Mary Austin Holley recounted how "Col. Travis ... when wounded and dying, was attacked by a Mexican officer who, in imitation of the western savage, seemed desirous of *'striking the body of the dead,'*—mustering his swiftly departing strength for one last act of noble daring, the brave Travis met and plunged his sword in the breast of the advancing enemy, and fell the victor with the victim, to rise no more." In 1841, Henry Stuart Foot—with more zeal than literary skill—told how "a Mexican general (Mora) then rushed upon [Travis] and lifted his sword to destroy his victim, who, collecting all his last expiring energies, directed a thrust at the former, which changed their relative positions; for the victim became the victor, and the remains of both descended to eternal sleep; but not alike to everlasting fame." In 1948, John Myers Myers stated that Travis "drove his sword through the Mexican, then fell with him." In 1958, Texas journalist Lon Tinkle in *13 Days to Glory*, Martha Anne Turner in her 1972 Travis biography, and Archie P. McDonald in 1976 all accepted the story.[17]

Significantly, Walter Lord's study did not contain the tale. Lord prudently chose not to included the incident, since primary evidence casts doubt upon the entire episode. When he seemed to have taken the story straight from Joe's lips, the sequence of events in the Gray version was strangely askew. As he told it, Travis sprang from his bed, mounted the wall, and was shot. At that point—immediately upon his master's fall—"Joe ... ran and ensconced himself in a house."[18] Presumably, the "house" was one of the rooms attached to the West Wall. Only afterward did Gray tell of the grappling match. But how did he know? His own narrative indicated that by the time the alleged Travis–Mora meeting, the slave was well "ensconced."

Childress provided a possible explanation. According to him, Joe talked with an English-speaking officer after the battle and it was from that conversation that "he knew his master had killed the general leading the siege, as their blood congealed together."[19]

Apparently, Joe had not actually seen the clash but accepted the officer's story. He told Gray that he was saved by a Captain Baragan (Gray's spelling?), but was he the same man who told him of his master's final gesture? Again, there is no way of knowing if any of this is really true.[20]

We do know, however, that Mexican reports discredit the notion that Mora was killed by Travis or anyone else. At the Alamo, acting general Ventura Mora commanded 280 troopers of the Permanent Cavalry Regiment of Dolores.[21] On one point all sources have agreed: Mexican cavalry units were stationed around the mission–fortress to cut down any Texians seeking escape.[22] Indeed, Sergeant Francisco Becerra specifically recalled Mora serving in that role.[23] While Mora seems to have been an intrepid officer, it is unlikely that a cavalry commander would have abandoned his mounted troopers to participate in an infantry assault. In addition, several Mexican combatants left accounts of the battle and not one recorded the death of a general. Surely, the loss of a general officer would have warranted at least a passing mention, especially when some, like Colonel José Enrique de la Peña, discussed casualty figures in some detail. Most significantly, Becerra recorded that *after* the battle, Santa Anna directed "Mora to send out his cavalry to bring in wood" to burn the bodies of the Alamo defenders.[24] Clearly, Travis had not killed General Mora.

Was it possible that Joe or Gray might have been mistaken about the name and that Travis could have killed some other Mexican officer? Even that is unlikely. The standard Mexican infantry musket, the 0.753 caliber Brown Bess, fired a huge lead ball over one-half inch in diameter. As Professor James W. Pohl and I have explained, "its massive slug was considerably larger than that of the heaviest machine gun currently in use."[25]

Can one reasonably believe that such a projectile penetrated Travis' head, sent him tumbling with the force of its blow, and then—with the round still embedded in his brain—he rallied, parried a lethal saber stroke, and responded with killing force? Highly improbable. Travis was formidable, but not superhuman.[26]

Someone obviously invented "poor Travis' last effort." But who and for what reason? Joe could have, but such a fabrication seems unlikely for one with his reputation for honesty; besides, what did he have to gain from such a tale? Childress suggested that the story stemmed from the unidentified Mexican officer who told it to Joe. Although Gray did not mention the Mexican, that would tend to explain the confused sequence of his narrative. What Childress did not explain was how this officer knew Travis from any other defender or the fact that no Mexican reports recorded the death of any general. One must finally conclude that what little evidence we have for the alleged Travis–Mora struggle is at least secondhand, and not at all credible.

Colonel Peña provided yet another version of Travis' death, but it disagrees with Joe's account. Peña described the scene after the Mexicans had breached the North Wall and the defenders were falling back helter-skelter to their secondary defenses in the Long Barracks: "Not all of [the Texians] took refuge, for some remained in the open, looking at us before firing, as if dumbfounded at our daring. Travis was seen to hesitate, but not about the death he would chose. He would take a few steps back and stop, turning his proud face towards us to discharge his shots; he fought like a true soldier. Finally, he died but after having traded his life very dearly."[27]

Even though Peña's is by far the most reliable of the Mexican accounts of the battle, his version of Travis' death is suspect. According to Joe, Travis was struck down before the Mexicans breached the North Wall. Peña has Travis alive and still fighting well after the Mexicans poured into the compound. Furthermore, Joe had his master defending and dying at the North Wall battery. Peña seems to place Travis on the "open" ground of the plaza after the North Wall had been abandoned. It would have been difficult for Travis to "take a few steps and stop" in the limited space of his battery. Finally, the question must be asked again: How was Peña able to identify Travis in the thick smoke of battle and early morning darkness. If Travis was generally known to the Mexicans why was Antonio Ruiz—who placed him on the north battery—required to identify his body after the battle. Some brave defender died as Peña described, but it was not Travis.

Texians steeped in nineteenth century romanticism welcomed the idea of a heroic death for the gallant Travis, and many of the romantic notions linger even in our own cynical time. In 1948, Myers argued that "the Alamo isn't a structure now; it is a symbol of valor in the minds of men."[28] More recently, Professor Paul A. Hutton of the University of New Mexico advanced the supposition that "the Alamo of our collective imagination has become dominant, assuming an importance in the national mind that is greater than that of the historical Alamo."[29]

The symbolic Travis has tended to obscure the real man; popular culture expects more from its heroes than a mere mortal can provide. Consequently, it invented a death for Travis that befitted a Texas Roland, a process that unfortunately robbed the man of his humanity. In the early morning darkness of March 6, 1836, Travis and some 188 other flesh-and-blood men heroically fought against overwhelming odds and died for the cause of Texas independence. When we forget that, in a real sense, we fail to "Remember the Alamo!"

Notes

1. Walter Lord, *A Time to Stand* (New York: Harper & Brothers, 1961), 155-156.

2. William Fairfax Gray, *From Virginia to Texas, 1835: Diary of Col. Wm. F. Gray, Giving Details of His Journey to Texas and Return in 1835-1836 And Second Journey to Texas in 1837* (Houston: The Fletcher Young Publishing Co., 1965), 137.

3. *Columbia* (Tennessee) *Observer*, April 14, 1836.

4. Sam Houston to Henry Raquet, March 13, 1836 in John H. Jenkins, ed., *The Papers of the Texas Revolution* (10 vols; Austin: Presidial Press, 1973), V, 71-72.

5. *Columbia* (Tennessee) *Observer*, April 14, 1836.

6. For a discussion of the Williams' dissertation, see Lord, *A Time to Stand*, 206. Ruiz did italicize the word "only"—i.e., Travis was "shot *only* in the forehead." That fact may have suggested suicide to Williams. Such a conclusion is, however, quite a leap of faith and most certainly runs contrary to Joe's account.

7. Francisco Antonio Ruiz, "The Fall of the Alamo," in *The Texas Almanac, 1857-1873, A Compendium of Texas History*, James M. Day, comp. (Waco, TX: Texian Press, 1967), 357.

8. *Fort Worth Gazette*, July 12, 1889.
9. *Ibid.*
10. Lord, *A Time to Stand*, 89-90.
11. *Fort Worth Gazette*, July 12, 1889.
12. Ruiz, "Fall of the Alamo," 357. Ruiz is clear on this point: "On the north battery of the fortress lay the lifeless body of Col. Travis . . ."
13. Lord, *A Time to Stand*, 205.
14. John J. Linn, *Reminiscences of Fifty Years in Texas* (New York: D. & J. Sadlier & Co., 1883), 141. John [Juan] Seguin, *Personal Memoirs of John N. Seguin, From the Year 1834 to the Retreat of General Woll from the City of San Antonio* (San Antonio: Ledger Book and Job Office, 1858),10. Seguin recalled "having met with Anselmo Vergara [Borgarra] and Andres Barcena, both soldiers of my company, whom I had left for the purpose of observation in the vicinity of San Antonio; they brought the intelligence of the fall of the Alamo."
15. Gray, *From Virginia to Texas*, 137.
16. *Columbia* (Tennessee) *Observer*, April 14, 1836.
17. Mary Austin Holley, *Texas* (Lexington, KY: J. Clarke & Co., 1836), 354. This is a much overlooked source that includes the first book printing of Travis' letter of February 24, 1836, as well as Houston's official report and many details on the Battle of San Jacinto; Henry Stuart Foote, *Texas and the Texans; or, Advance of the Anglo-Americans to the South-West; Including a History of Leading Events in Mexico, From the Conquest by Fernando Cortes to the Termination of the Texan Revolution* (Philadelphia: Thomas, Cowperthwait & Co., 1841), 223; John Myers Myers, *The Alamo* (New York: E. P. Dutton & Company, Inc., 1948), 20; Lon Tinkle, *Thirteen Days to Glory* (New York: McGraw-Hill Book Company, Inc., 1958), 211; Martha Anne Turner, *William Barret Travis: His Sword And His Pen* (Waco: Texian Press, 1972), 250; Archie P. McDonald, *Travis* (Austin: Jenkins Publishing Co., 1976), 176.

While I differ with Professor McDonald's interpretation of this minor point, in all fairness, it must be admitted that his Travis is the best biography of the man. McDonald, in the words of one reviewer, "makes a man of flesh out of a statue," In his 1976 biography he related how "A Mexican officer tried to bayonet him, but Travis, with a final effort, ran him through with a sword," but in his most recent study, *Travis: One Chief Rol'd Among the Rest* (Victoria: TX: The Victoria College Press, 1986), he maintains only that "Travis died early in the assault, a single bullet piercing his head," (p. 14) seemingly rejecting the death struggle. Some later writers added a new twist to the fable. Tinkle, for example, indicated that Travis "was pierced himself while piercing [Mora], the two officers expiring together." Ruiz's observation that Travis was shot "*only*" through the forehead—with no mention of a saber wound—would seem to discredit that particular variation of the story. In fact, the *alcalde* may have already heard it, which would explain his emphasis on the word "only."

18. Gray, *From Virginia to Texas*, 137.
19. *Columbia* (Tennessee) *Observer*, April 14, 1836.
20. Vicente Filisola, *Memoirs for the History of the War in Texas*, Wallace Woolsey, trans. (2 vols.; Austin: Eakin Press, 1987), II 5, 73, 90, 92; José Enrique de la Peña, *With Santa Anna in Texas: A Personal Narrative of the Revolution* (College Station: Texas A&M Press, 1975), 116, 127, 148. I have

been unsuccessful in establishing the identity of Joe's savior. General Filisola mentioned a Captain Manuel Barragan, a commander of presidial dragoons. According to Filisola, he commanded a cannon during the siege in Bexar but later deserted with his entire company on December 10, 1835. Colonel Peña, on the other hand, mentions a Marcos Barragan who was also a captain of presidial soldiers. According to Peña, Marcos Barragan became an aide to general Santa Anna. This was probably the same man but either Filisola or Peña got the first name wrong. If Captain Barragan had been stationed in a Texas presidio prior to the war, there was a good chance he may have come in contact with some of the American settlers and hence picked up some English. Filisola wrote that "Captain Manuel Barragan and an escort from the presidio company of Lampazos" accompanied Stephen F. Austin from Matamoros to Mexico City during the time he was under arrest in 1834. if this is indeed the same man who saved Joe he may have learned a little English from Austin or others. Austin, of course, would have had no need of an English-speaking escort since he spoke fluent Spanish by that time.

21. Filisola, *War in Texas*, 149; the Mexican order of battle is also listed in Richard G. Santos, *Santa Anna's Campaign Against Texas, 1835-1836* (Waco, TX: Texian Press, 1968), 14.

22. Santa Anna Order, March 5, 1836, in John H. Jenkins, ed., *The Papers of the Texas Revolution, 1835-1836* (10 vols., Austin, TX: Presidial Press, 1973), IV, 518-519. In this, the most primary of all the references to the horsemen around the mission–fortress, Santa Anna ordered "the cavalry, under Joaquin Ramirez y Sesma, will be stationed at the Alameda, saddling at 3 o'clock A.M. It shall be its duty to scout the country, to prevent the possibility of escape."

23. Francisco Becerra, *A Mexican Sergeant's Recollections of the Alamo & San Jacinto*, John S. Ford, ed., Austin, TX: Jenkins Publishing Company, 1980), 18. Becerra remembered Mora as a colonel, but that was a natural mistake as he told his tale thirty-nine years later after the fact, and Mora led a regiment, which normally would have been commanded by a colonel. Furthermore, Filisola lists Mora as an "acting" general; after the disastrous war in Texas his rank may well have reverted to colonel. In my view the Becerra account has taken a "bum rap." In 1961, Walter Lord labeled it "probably the least reliable of all the Mexican accounts" in *A Time to Stand* (p. 227). Ever since, the Becerra narrative had been widely ignored. Granted, his account of the deaths of Travis, Crockett and Bowie must be dismissed as total buncombe. Elsewhere, however, Becerra seems fairly accurate and provides many useful details of the battle. Like all primary materials, Becerra must be used with equal measures of caution and judgment, but on the whole he seems more reliable than Nunez, who Lord seems to have accepted without question.

24. Becerra, *Recollections of the Alamo & San Jacinto*, 24.

25. James W. Pohl and Stephen L. Hardin, "The Military History of the Texas Revolution: An Overview," *Southwestern Historical Quarterly*, LXXXIX (January 1986), 280.

26. I have discussed this question with a physician friend of mine who assures me that the case books abound with examples of those with massive head wounds who rallied to perform seemingly incredible feats. So be it. I do not

argue that "Travis' last effort" is impossible, only that it was highly unlikely and—most important—that there is no eyewitness evidence to support it.

27. Peña, *With Santa Anna in Texas*, 50.
28. Myers, *The Alamo*, 235.
29. Paul Andrew Hutton, "Introduction," in Susan Prendergast Schoelwer with Tom W. Glaser, *Alamo Images: Changing Perceptions of a Texas Experience* (Dallas: DeGolyer Library and Southern Methodist University Press, 1985), 4.

ABOUT THE ARTICLE'S AUTHOR

Dr. Stephen L. Hardin

Dr. Stephen L. Hardin earned his Ph.D. at Texas Christian University in 1989. He has taught for the last decade at The Victoria College in Victoria, Texas, where he is a member of the school's Department of Social Sciences.

He has written several books but his most acclaimed volume is *Texian Iliad: A Military History of the Texas Revolution, 1835-1836*. The 1994 publication earned a number of awards including the 1994 T. R. Fehrenbach Award, and the 1995 Kate Broocks Bates Award for Historical Research. *Texian Iliad* also won the Westerners International Co-Founders Book Award, first prize for Best Non-Fiction Book Published in 1994, and was listed among the "Ten Best Texas Books" by the *Austin Chronicle* in 1996.

Hardin has written articles for several publications including *Military Illustrated*, the *Southwestern Historical Quarterly*, *The Journal of South Texas*, and the *East Texas Historical Journal*, among others.

Dr. Hardin has been involved in a number of Alamo-related projects. He served as an on-camera commentator in "The Battle of the Alamo" segment of the Arts & Entertainment network's *The Real West* series, and several other History Channel programs. More recently, he was the historical advisor for *The Alamo* (2004).

In March 1989, Hardin delivered a paper, "J. C. Neill: The Forgotten Alamo Commander," at the annual Alamo Society Symposium. The paper was subsequently printed in issue no. 66 of *The Alamo Journal*.

Earlier, in December 1987, Dr. Hardin penned "A Volley from the Darkness: Sources Regarding the Death of William Barret Travis" for issue no. 59 of *The Alamo Journal*.

ABOUT THE ARTIST

Gary S. Zaboly

Gary S. Zaboly is a New York-based military illustrator who created his first *Alamo Journal* cover in May 1992 for issue no. 81. Over the years, his artwork has graced the covers of many *Alamo Journal* issues.

He is the author of *A True Ranger: The Life and Many Wars of Major Robert Rogers*, and *American Colonial Ranger: The Northern Colonies 1724-64*.

Zaboly has created illustrations for a number of historical publications including *American History Illustrated*, *Muzzle Blasts*, *Military Collector and Historian*, *True West*, *Civil War Times*, *Muzzleloader*, *French and Indian War Magazine*, and the *Bulletin of the Fort Ticonderoga Museum*, among others.

A number of books have featured his artwork including *The Alamo Almanac And Book of Lists*, *Blood of Noble Men: The Alamo Siege and Battle*, *Texian Iliad*, and *The Davy Crockett Almanac And Book of Lists*.

He also provided illustrations for *The French and Indian War: America's First World War*, *The Gates of the Alamo*, *Chronicles of Lake Champlain*, *The United States Infantry: An Illustrated History, 1775-1918*, and *The Annotated and Illustrated Journals of Major Robert Rogers*.

Zaboly has painted covers for several books including *Texas and Texans in the Civil War*, *Custer and His Times*, and *Warriors of Lincoln County*, among others.

His work has appeared in such televison productions as *American Heritage Presents: The Alamo*, the Arts & Entertainment network's *The Real West*, the History Channel's *This Week in History*, and *Frontier: The Decisive Battles*, among others.

Millions of visitors to the Alamo in San Antonio have viewed Zaboly's detailed illustrations on various orientation markers, and on the Shrine of Texas Liberty's Wall of History.

"The Long Ride Home" by Gary Zaboly, Alamo Journal, no. 118 (September 2000)

Courage Under Fire: The Mexican Army at the Battle of the Alamo

by William R. Chemerka

History and popular culture have paid constant homage to the defenders of the Alamo who died for liberty and freedom during the predawn darkness of the famous March 6, 1836, battle. Books, poems, songs, paintings, lithographs, and motion pictures have celebrated the courage of that gallant garrison for over 150 years. To be sure, the names of such defenders as David Crockett, James Bowie and William Barret Travis are well known. And certainly the likes of James Butler Bonham, Almeron Dickinson and Green B. Jameson, among many others, are nearly as identifiable as Crockett, Bowie, and Travis to those who have studied the Texas Revolution. Through the efforts of historians, both professional and amateur, at least 189 defenders—both Anglo and Tejano—who perished in the defense of Texas, have been identified by name.

Of course, the Tejano defenders—Juan Abamillo, Juan Badillo, Carlos Espalier, Gregorio Esparza, Antonio Fuentes, José M. Guerrero, Damacio Jimenez, Toribio Losoya, and Andres Nava—are equals to Crockett, Bowie, Travis and the others in the halls of Alamo bravery. Over the last two decades, San Antonio's active Latino community appropriately focused its attention toward properly acknowledging the historical contributions of the Tejanos during the Alamo's thirteen days of glory. For example, on November 30, 1986, the same year of the Texas Sesquicentennial, a life-sized action sculpture of Toribio Losoya was unveiled in ceremonies on the Paseo del Alamo, just yards away from where the Alamo's West Wall once stood. Created by sculptor William Easley, the bronze figure of Losoya is depicted holding the Mexican Constitutional flag of 1824 in his left hand while pointing a flintlock pistol in his right.[1] Students of the Texas Revolution can look at both David Crockett and Toribio Losoya as men of conviction, honor and courage.

But what of those other participants in the struggle for historical recognition: the Mexican soldado who besieged and attacked the Alamo. Those seemingly anonymous soldiers suffered greatly and are worthy of history's attention.

Following the defeat of Gen. Martin Perfecto de Cos' command in San Antonio de Bexar by Texian revolutionaries in early December 1835, Santa Anna quickly organized a large army to quell the growing insurrection in Texas. The Mexican Army departed from the heart of its homeland in late 1835. San Luis Potosi was a starting point for much of the army. Later, when his command arrived northward at Saltillo, his battlefield units were organized for the invasion of San Antonio e Bexar, nearly 400 miles away.

Although there were some qualified officers—generals José Urrea and Ramirez y Sesma—among his leadership corps, his enlisted ranks suffered from an inconsistency of quality. Clearly, the infantry battalions needed to be filled, but by whom? "Privates were hard to catch. Bad leadership, poor pay and no glory were all that waited them."[2] As a result, some infantry units were not organized at full strength. "Local officials [had] scraped the barrel to fill their quotas."[3] Santa Anna's army had been subsequently filled by Indians, recently liberated convicts and unskilled conscripts. Yet the army included the relatively well-trained Zapadores battalion and the permanent Tampico regiment. To be sure, it was an army of diverse talents, skills and backgrounds.

Santa Anna informed Gen. Vicente Filisola on December 23, 1835, that he had secured enough supplies for his army through Col. Ricardo Dromundo, Purveyor of the Army of Operations.

The commander in chief requested "one thousand cargas of flour, one thousand of corn, beans, rice, lard, and salt, so that there shall be rations for two months supply for six thousand men."[4] Despite the order for provisions, distribution problems arose on the march. One Mexican officer, Lt. Col. José Enrique de la Peña, reported that "necessities had been poorly estimated and incompetent management caused many of the supplies to be lost, for in trying to save ten a hundred would be lost. Items such as crackers, rice and salt, which should have been transported in barrels or boxes were carried in gunny sacks, so that the rains [sic] or the ropes that held the loads to an animal ruined them."[5] Even the Mexican commander noted "the scarcity of supplies...."[6]

And no soldier in Santa Anna's command was prepared for the winter weather that awaited them. The severely harsh winter played havoc with the Mexican troops. "The snowfall increased and kept falling in great abundance, so continuous that at dawn it was knee-deep," noted de la Peña. "Indeed, one could not remain standing or sitting, much less lying down; those not taking care to shake their clothes frequently soon were numb with cold and, immobilized by the weight that had been added to their bodies, were obliged to beg the help of others in order to move, but help was given only with great reluctance."[7]

Furthermore, illness—primarily dysentery—and desertion helped reduce Santa Anna's army by some 500 soldiers prior to the force's arrival in Bexar in February. Yet these trying circumstances should not have surprised the so-called Napoleon of the West. In fact, Gen. Martin Perfecto de Cos' march to Bexar months earlier was marked by similar tragedies. In his published work, *The Texas War*, Carlos Sanchez-Navarro identified some of Cos' soldiers who had perished on the march prior to the Battle of Bexar in December 1835. On November 26, 1835, for example, the likes of Juan Evaristo, Victor Garcia and Guadalupe Salcido died as faithful, dutiful soldiers.[8] Unfortunately, their names do not appear on any honor roll.

Santa Anna's army continued northward. Compounding the army's problem was the large number of camp followers—

women and children—who accompanied the men in uniform. "[They also] had to be fed, and they shared the small pittances doled out as rations to the soldiers."[9] Like the soldiers, they suffered accordingly. "Of the 1,500 camp followers ... who left Laredo with the army, less than 300 reached Bexar. They died of hunger, thirst and exposure by the wayside."[10]

Yet, the army marched on. "With the stoicism of all soldiers in all armies, most of the men somehow carried on."[11] Lacking adequate materialistic provisions, one might assume that Santa Anna would have at least provided for his Catholic troops' spiritual needs. However, "in all the army," lamented General Vicente Filisola, Santa Anna's second in command, "there was not a single chaplain for the spiritual aid and comfort for the religious minded men in their troubles."[12]

The problems of the troublesome march were so widespread that seemingly everyone was aware of them. Ramon Caro, Santa Anna's secretary remembered "a poor wretch whom we found, at the point of death, unable to move, loaded down with his gun and pack. We placed him in one of the wagons, but he expired before the day's journey was over. Of course, he, like many others, received no spiritual consultation. Such was the sad spectacle offered by the army on its march."[13]

Only ten days before advance units of the Mexican Army reached San Antonio de Bexar, a blizzard exploded upon the landscape. The snowfall slowed the army's march and its ability to establish nightly camps. Comfort was never something a soldier in the field expected but the lack of basic essentials was extremely problematic. Firewood became difficult to find and even more difficult to ignite. Mules, horses, oxen, soldados and camp followers suffered and died.

However, in Santa Anna's eyes the army remained upbeat, steadfast and eager to achieve its goals. Reports from his officers reinforced the general's optimistic views. For example, in a letter written to Santa Anna by Gen. José Urrea, commander of the Army of Operations at Goliad, on February 27, 1836: "I ... conclude in assuring you that the soldiers composing this division are fraught with enthusiasm; and burn to distinguish themselves in defence of the sacred rights of the nation."[14] According to Santa Anna, this collective expression of confidence and martial enthusiasm would manifest itself in the predawn assault on the Alamo.

According to Santa Anna, his army was expected to be the instrument of his will in defeating the rebellious Texians. Noted the commander-in-chief on March 3, 1836: "Foreigners invading the republic and taken with arms in their hands shall be judged and treated as pirates."[15] Furthermore, Santa Anna, distastefully characterized the rebellious Tejanos as "unnatural Mexicans."[16]

Santa Anna's zealous disdain for the revolutionaries and his army's resilience resulted in a formidable combination. On March 5, 1836, Santa Anna delivered his orders of attack for the following morning: Four infantry columns, all equipped with ladders and some with crowbars and axes. "The arms, principally the bayonet, should be in perfect order," stated the general. Unfortunately, the care and comfort of his enlisted and conscripted men were not priorities. Despite the early March cold, to say nothing of what the Mexican Army had suffered in its trek to Bexar, Santa Anna ordered that "the men will wear neither overcoats nor blankets, or anything that may impede the rapidity of their movements."[17] And to their credit, the Mexican soldados—underpaid, underfed and ill-provisioned—carried out Santa Anna's battle plan the following morning.

De la Peña recalled how his fellow soldiers behaved immediately prior to the attack. "Our soldiers, it was said, lacked the cool courage that is demanded by an assault, but they were steadfast and the survivors will have nothing to be ashamed of. Each one individually confronted and prepared his soul for the terrible moment, expressed his last wishes and silently and cooly took those steps which preceded an encounter."[18]

And what a bloody encounter it was!

Remarked de la Peña: "The columns, bravely storming the fort in the midst of a terrible shower of bullets and cannon fire ... The few poor ladders that we were bringing had not arrived, because their bearers had either perished or had escaped. But the courage of our soldiers was not diminished as they saw their comrades falling dead or wounded."[19]

The soldados in the front ranks were particularly vulnerable from Texian musket and rifle as they approached the Alamo's outer walls. Some of these men were even accidentally killed by their fellow soldiers in the predawn mayhem. However, most initial Mexican casualties resulted from artillery fire. Cannon blasts, especially those volleys filled with canister shot, took their toll with horrific effectiveness.

Mexican infantrymen who scaled the ladders first were, of course, likely to receive the swift swing of a musket butt or the quick slash from a knife or tomahawk blade. The fighting—again, in the the dark—was hellish. Muzzleloaders flashing, some at point blank range, frequently found their marks on both sides of the Alamo's old walls.

The soldados "were hit by a hail of shrapnel and bullets that the besieged men let loose on them."[20] One cannon volley "opened a lane in our lines at least fifty feet broad."[21]

De la Peña again used the term *courage* to describe the attack as it shifted from the walls to the Long Barracks. "Our soldiers," he wrote, "some stimulated by courage and others by fury, burst into the quarters where the enemy had entrenched themselves, from which issued an infernal fire. Behind these came others, who, nearing the doors and blind with fury and smoke, fired their shots against friends and enemies alike, and in this way our losses were most grievous."[22] Eventually, noted de la Peña, "death united, in one place, both friends and enemies."[23]

Said Sergeant Becerra: "Our soldiers, inspired by success, continued to attack with energy and boldness. The Texians fought like devils. It was short range—muzzle-to-muzzle—hand-to-hand—musket-and-rifle—and Bowie knife—all were mingled in confusion. Here a squad of Mexicans, there a Texian or two. The crash of firearms, the shouts of defiance, the cries of the dying and the wounded, made a din almost infernal."[24]

Still, de la Peña criticized the operation, which resulted in so many infantry casualties. "What had been the use of bringing up the artillery if it were not to be used ... ? We should we have been forced to leap over a fortified place? Why, before agreeing on the sacrifice, which was great indeed, had no one borne in his mind that we had no means at our disposal to save our wounded?"[25]

Dead and wounded soldados littered the battlefield. Some died quickly while others languished for hours before their ultimate fate was sealed. Following the burning of the Texian dead, a number of the dead Mexican soldiers were buried. However, due to the large number of Mexican dead many of them were thrown into the San Antonio River.

On March 6 of each year, as we appropriately remember the Alamo and its defenders, some reflection should focus on their adversaries, particularly the faceless enlisted men in the Mexican Army of Operations. There is no roll call for those Mexican soldiers who faced death, only sincere consideration by those of us who care to remember.

Notes

1. A news release folder, which accompanied the unveiling of the 300-pound bronze creation, acknowledged the increasing historical importance of the Lone Star State's Hispanic community: "The sculpture is a gift to the people of San Antonio and Texas from the Adolph Coors Company as a lasting symbol of the many contributions made by Hispanics in the development of Texas and the United States."

2. Walter Lord, *A Time to Stand* (Harper & Bros., New York, 1961), 66.

3. *Ibid.*

4. Santa Anna to Filisola, Dec. 23, 1835, in John H. Jenkins, ed., *The Papers of the Texas Revolution*, Presidial Pres, Austin, TX (1973) Vol. III, 303.

5. *With Santa Anna in Texas; A Personal Narrative of the Revolution by Jose´Enrique de la Peña*, Carmen Perry, trans, Texas A&M University Press, College Station, TX. 1975, 19-20.

6. Santa Anna to Filisola, Dec. 28, 1835, in Jenkins, *Papers*, Vol. III, 353.

7. *With Santa Anna in Texas*, 27.

8. Carlos Sanchez-Navarro y Peon, *La Guerra de Tejas; Memorias de un Soldado* (Mexico: Editorial Polis, 1938),

9. James T. DeShields, *Tall Men With Long Rifles* (The Naylor Co., San Antonio, TX. 1971),102.

10. *Ibid.*

11. Lord, 73.

12. Don Vicente Filisola, *Memoirs For The History Of The War In Texas*, (Eakin Press: Austin, TX, 1987), Vol. II, 153.

13. Ramon Martinez Caro, *Verdadera Idea De La Primera Campaña De Tejas y Sucesos Ocurridos Despues De La Accion De San Jacinto* (Mexico: Imprenta de Santiago Perez, 1837) printed in Carlos E. Castaneda, trans., *The Mexican Side of the Texas Revolution* (New York: Arno Press, 1976), 101.

14. Urrea to Santa Anna, Feb. 27, 1836 in Jenkins, *Papers*, Vol. IV, 451-452.
15. Santa Anna to Urrea, March 3, 1836 in Jenkins, *Papers*, Vol. IV, 501.
16. *Ibid.*
17. Santa Anna Order, March 5, 1836, in Jenkins, *Papers*, Vol. IV, 519.
18. *With Santa Anna in Texas*, 45.
19. *Ibid.*, 48.
20. Filisola, *Memoirs*, Vol. II, 177.
21. "The Felix Nuñez Account and the Siege of the Alamo: A Critical Appraisal," Edited by Stephen L. Hardin in *Southwestern Historical Quarterly*, Vo. XCIV, No. 1 (July, 1990), 78. Although the volley of a single cannon could not create a fifty-foot-wide opening in the Mexican lines, a battery of guns could accomplish such a task.
22. *With Santa Anna in Texas*, 50.
23. *Ibid.*, 54.
24. Francisco Becerra, *A Mexican Sergeant's Recollections of the Alamo and San Jacinto*, Austin: Jenkins Publishing Co., 1980, 21.
25. *With Santa Anna in Texas*, 55.

ABOUT THE ARTICLE'S AUTHOR

William R. Chemerka

William R. Chemerka is the founder of The Alamo Society, and editor of its quarterly publication, *The Alamo Journal*.

He is the author of *The Alamo Almanac and Book of Lists* (Eakin Press, 1997) and *The Davy Crockett Almanac and Book of Lists* (Eakin Press, 2000). Chemerka is the editor of *The Crockett Chronicle*, a quarterly dedicated to the life and legend of David Crockett. He is also contributing editor at *New Jersey Heritage Magazine*, and has written for *The Star-Ledger*.

Chemerka has appeared as a historical commentator on The History Channel, the Arts and Entertainment Network, C-SPAN Book TV and WCCO (CBS) radio. He was a writer for The History Channel's *First Invasion: The War of 1812*, and served as the featured historian on the Biography Channel's 2002 live webcast, *Live From Austin: The Story of Davy Crockett*.

In 2004, *Texas Monthly* dubbed Chemerka "the Google of Alamo buffs."

Chemerka is a multi-award-winning educator, and is recognized by "Who's Who Among American Teachers." He teaches at The Humanities Center in Peapack-Gladstone, New Jersey, and is a speaker for Americana Lectures.

Chemerka is a member of the Texas State Historical Association, the Company of Military Historians, the Brigade of the American Revolution, the New Jersey Historical Society, the Screen Actors Guild, and the Actor's Equity Association.

"1824 Flag" by William R. Chemerka, Alamo Journal, no. 53 (December 1986)

Where Did The 1824 Flag Fly?

by Bill Walraven

On the assumption that (1) Texas had not declared its independence and (2) the Federalist 1824 symbol would probably elicit support from some of Santa Anna's followers, historians have argued that the banner flying over the Alamo on March 6, 1836, was the flag of the Mexican Constitution of 1824. Quite likely that is not the case.

Rueben Marmaduke Potter is generally credited with being the first to offer the Flag of 1824 thesis when he wrote in 1860: "It is a fact not often remembered that Travis and his band fell under the Mexican Federal Flag of 1824 instead of the Lone Star of Texas, although Independence, unknown to them, had been declared by the new convention four days before at Washington-on-the-Brazos. They died for a Republic whose existence they never knew."

However, the 1824 flag story may have an even earlier source. Joseph Hefter, an authority on Mexican history originally published *The Siege and Taking of the Alamo* for Gen. Sanchez Lamego, a Mexican military historian. In the English translation of the book, he quoted British historian William Kennedy in *Texas* (New York, 1844), Vol. II, pages 180-181: "It must be kept well in mind that Texas Independence had not yet been declared, and that the defenders of the Alamo fought under the Mexican Federal flag of 1824." Note the similarity between the comment and Potter's. The passage does not appear in Kennedy's first edition, published in 1841 in London.

Regardless of the originator of the 1824 theory, others followed suit. Amelia Williams, in her 1934 study, *A Critical Study of the Siege of the Alamo and of the Personnel of Its Defenders*, said: "Yoakum, Potter, H. A. McArdle and other more recent students agree that the Alamo flag was the Mexican tricolor with the numerals 1824 on the white bar ... This flag was almost certainly the one used at the Alamo."

J. Frank Dobie in *No Help for the Alamo*, said: "Contrary to popular belief, the Texans did not fly a Lone Star, but a tricolored green, white and red Mexican flag with 1824 stitched across the white stripe."

Historian John Henry Brown, who wrote *History of Texas*, agreed. An 1885 painting by French artist Jean Louis Theodore Gentilz shows the 1824 flag, twenty-five years after the Potter myth was planted.

However, current thinking does not favor the flag. In *A Time to Stand*, author Walter Lord said: "Texas stopped fighting for the Constitution of 1824 long before the Alamo ... early in 1836 popular opinion swung violently and overwhelming for independence.... Down came the old 1824 flags."

Three days before the battle, Alamo commander William Barret Travis wrote to Jesse Grimes: "... under the flag of independence, we are ready to peril our lives a hundred times a day."

The history of the 1824 flag begins with Philip Dimmitt, commander of the fortress La Bahia. On October 17, 1835, he wrote to Stephen F. Austin: "I have had a flag made—the colours and their arrangement the same as the old one—with the words and figures, 'Constitution of 1824' displayed on the white in the centre."

At this time Dimmitt and Austin were both supporters of the federalist cause. Dimmitt suggested the flag as he proposed an invasion of Matamoros, Mexico, where he believed Mexican Federalists would join the cause.

It is probable that Dimmitt carried his banner to San Antonio, where he and his men participated in the Storming of Bexar in December of 1835. He knew that some 250 cavalrymen under Gen. Martin Perfecto de Cos' command in Bexar had served under Col. José Maria Gonzales and were sympathetic to the liberal cause.

However, something he saw in that battle changed Dimmitt's mind. He returned to Goliad firmly convinced any further liaison with the federalists in Mexico was hopeless, for they were nationalists first and were changing sides to combat the American invaders. Dimmitt said it would be victory or death—no quarter.

It is highly likely that Dimmitt left the red, white and green banner at the Alamo because back at Goliad he constructed the first flag of independence, which featured a bloody arm holding a sword. Dimmitt may have borrowed the symbol from Capt. William S. Brown, who served in his command and later displayed a similar flag at Washington-on-the-Brazos. The flag was raised over La Bahia in conjunction with the signing of a premature Declaration of Independence there on December 20, 1835.

Though he credited Dimmitt with the creation of the 1824 flag, Refugio historian Hobart Huson assumed that it was used by the defenders of the Alamo when it fell. This impression may have been created by the fact that the red, white, and green flag probably flew over the Alamo as late as December 30, 1835, when Dr. James Grant embarked on an ill-fated expedition to invade Matamoros.

The young German volunteer, Herman Ehrenberg, joined Grant on that venture. Shortly before the departure, Ehrenberg wrote: "We still considered Texas and Mexico as one ... three colors floated over the church."

When Grant stripped the Alamo of blankets, gunpowder, and other supplies that would be vitally missed two months later, he would have also taken the 1824 flag. Grant was not in favor of independence. He was more interested in regaining his land holdings in Mexico than in a revolt for patriotic reasons.

On January 10, 1836, Col. F. W. Johnson wrote of the Matamoros expedition: "The Federal Volunteer army of Texas ... under the command of Francis W. Johnson ... march under the flag of 1-8-2-4."

When the volunteers reached Goliad, Dr. Grant was incensed at Dimmitt's flag of independence. Dimmitt lowered his flag only after an armed confrontation was threatened. A report by Irish empressario James McGloin described the clash and quoted Johnson and Grant as "stating that they were Federalists and would stand for the Constitution of 1824."

Grant commandeered three month's supplies, which the garrison could ill afford to provide. He also took the garrison's entire *caballarda*, or herd of working horses, a condition that was to hinder James Fannin's defense of the Goliad fortress in the months ahead.

When the expedition reached Refugio, Sam Houston harangued the troops and convinced all but sixty of the some 450 that a Matamoros invasion was not a good idea.

Johnson and Grant continued on to San Patricio. Then, on February 27, 1836, Gen. José Urrea's army caught Johnson's group sleeping and killed or captured most of them. However, Johnson and several others escaped.

On March 2, Urrea set up an ambush on Agua Dulce Creek and killed Grant and a number of his men. Others were captured and sent to Matamoros as prisoners along with those from San Patricio.

Potter, who was in Matamoros, talked to the prisoners and worked to gain their release. In 1878 he wrote that by the end of February 1836, Grant "was probably the only armed Texan who still harbored any hope for the Constitution of 1824 or any wish to prolong the union with Mexico." He also said that Grant's men "had been taken under the flag of 1824."

Since Grant was on a horse-hunting expedition, it is unlikely that he had a flag when he was ambushed. He would have left it at San Patricio, where Johnson and the other contingent waited for him.

General Urrea's report stated: "The enemy was attacked at half past three in the morning in the midst of the rain, and although forty men within the fort defended themselves resolutely, the door was forced at dawn, sixteen being killed and twenty-four being taken prisoners. The town and the rest of the inhabitants did not suffer the least damage. I captured a flag and all kinds of arms and ammunition."

Urrea did not describe the flag he captured, even though he had been a Federalist before the invasion of Texas. A "Constitution of 1824" flag would have enraged Gen. Santa Anna, for it would have been even more unpopular among the Centralist regime than among the Texians.

The evidence is circumstantial, but the strongest case is that the Constitution of 1824 banner was captured at San Patricio and did not fly above the Alamo eight days later.

ABOUT THE ARTICLE'S AUTHOR

William Walraven

William Walraven, a native Texan, graduated with a journalism–history degree from Texas A&I College in Kingsville, Texas, and attended the University of Oklahoma.

He spent thirty-seven years in the newspaper business working for such publications as the *San Antonio Light*, the *San Antonio Express-News* and the *Corpus Christi Caller-Times*. Twenty-two of those journalistic years were devoted to writing a daily column on topics ranging from history to humor.

He has written eight books including *Corpus Christi: History of a Texas Seaport*, *Real Texans Don't Drink Scotch in Their Dr. Pepper*, *All I Know Is What's on TV* and *Walraven's World*, among others. Along with his wife, Marjorie, Walraven has written *The Magnificent Barbarians: Little-Told Tales of the Texas Revolution*, *Gift of the Wind: The Corpus Christi Bayfront*, and *Empresarios' Children: The Welders of Texas*, which weaves the story of a pioneer ranching family whose Texas roots go back to 1807.

The Walraven's *Magnificent Barbarians: Little-Told Tales of the Texas Revolution*, is particularly important since it carries a listing of United States troops who actively participated in the Texas Revolution. By comparing returns and rosters of the Third and Sixth Infantry Regiments at Fort Jesup in Louisiana with Texas rosters and land grants, the Walravens show that there was considerable United States presence in the revolution.

"Where Did the 1824 Flag Fly?" originally appeared in issue no. 77 (June/July 1991) of *The Alamo Journal*. The article subsequently appeared in *The Magnificent Barbarians: Little-Told Tales of the Texas Revolution*.

"And on the Fatal Third Time" by John Bourdage, Alamo Journal, no. 63 (October 1998).

James Butler Bonham
Oct. 17, 1835-March 6, 1836

Thomas Ricks Lindley

"Faster than a speeding bullet, more powerful than a locomotive, able to leap tall buildings at a single bound" were the words used to open the Superman TV series from the 1950s. Had the terms existed when Seth Shepard gave a speech on the Battle of the Alamo to the San Marcos Chautauqua Assembly on July 8, 1889, he would have probably chosen them to describe Alamo defender James Butler Bonham. Instead, Shepard used the words of a Texas newspaper man-historian-Indian fighter John Henry Brown to paint a dramatic picture of Bonham's return to the Alamo on the morning of March 3, 1836.[1]

According to Brown, writing for the May 15, 1889, issue of *Farm and Ranch*, and other writers who accept Brown's version, Bonham returned to the Alamo with Samuel A. Maverick and John W. Smith. The men are alleged to have halted on a hilltop overlooking San Antonio and saw that the Alamo was doomed. Maverick and Smith are supposed to have urged Bonham to retreat with them as any attempt to enter the Alamo at that point was sure death. Bonham is said to have answered: "I will report the result of my mission or die in the attempt." Then with a white handkerchief in his hat, a prearranged signal with Travis, and riding a cream-white horse, Bonham rode through the Mexican lines to enter the Alamo while Maverick and Smith departed with their lives.[2]

What information was so important that Bonham was willing

to risk his life to report it to Travis? Without exception, Alamo historians believe Bonham returned to tell Travis there would be no help coming from Goliad or Gonzales. Because of that sacrifice, Bonham occupies the number four hero "slot" among Alamo defenders behind David Crockett, James Bowie, and William Barret Travis.

Bonham's road to Texas and immortality began in Mobile, Alabama, on October 17, 1835, at the Shakespeare Theater where he led a rally supporting the Texian cause. Later, at a second rally, he was selected by Mobile citizens to carry their resolutions of support to General Sam Houston. Bonham's next action to stoke the fire of the building supernova was his part in the organization of the Mobile Greys military unit.[3]

Arriving in Texas too late to reach Bexar and take part in the December victory over Mexican forces, Bonham separated from the Greys and approached Sam Houston. On December 1, 1835, at San Felipe, Bonham put pen to paper and wrote what appears to be a self-serving introduction to General Sam Houston. It reads: "Permit me, through you to volunteer my services in the present struggle of Texas without conditions. I shall receive nothing, either in the form of service pay, or lands, or rations. Yours with great regards, James Butler Bonham. P.S. Will you, if you please, do me the kindship of showing this letter at any leisure moment, to his excellency the Gov. [—] J. B. B."[4]

Houston, who early in his career had taken the same track with General Andrew Jackson, without doubt took a liking to the young lawyer from South Carolina and Alabama. On December 20, 1835, Bonham received a commission as a cavalry lieutenant.[5] It does not appear that he was assigned to any specific unit because in January 1836 he was free enough to set up a law practice in Brazoria. In doing this, Bonham placed the following announcement in the *Texas Telegraph and Register*:[6] "LAW NOTICE—The subscriber will open a law office in Brazoria to receive such business as he may be favored with in his profession. He has with him licenses to practice law in South Carolina and Alabama of the United States of the North."

According to author Lon Tinkle, Bonham next joined Travis in running the Texas recruiting service. Also, around that time, Tinkle said Houston recommended to the provisional government's council that Bonham be promoted to major, but the request was turned down due to the council's hostility toward Houston.[7] On January 17, 1836, Houston, while at Goliad, sent James Bowie to Bexar to inspect the Alamo and to decide if it should be defended or abandoned. While Houston wanted the old mission closed down and destroyed, he left it up to Bowie to make the final decision. Historians claim Bonham entered the Alamo as a member of Bowie's small detachment.

Dr. John Sutherland, Travis' messenger to Gonzales on February 23, 1836, wrote that while Bonham was ready to join the army at Bexar when needed, he was holding himself in reserve when the Mexican army marched into Bexar.[8] Travis, in his letter of March 3, 1836, first identified Bonham as "Colonel J. B. Bonham (courier from Gonzales)." Later in the letter, Travis described Bonham as "my special messenger." Bonham had been a colonel of artillery in South Carolina as a military aide to the governor, but there is no evidence he was ever a colonel in the Texas army. The title of "special messenger," the failure of Travis and others to address Bonham according to his actual rank, and the fact that he had time to set up a law office, suggest Bonham may have enjoyed some kind of special reserve status, possibly due to his relationship with Houston.

Regardless of Bonham's exact military status, he was at the Alamo in late January 1836. On the 26th of January, he was selected as chairman of a committee to draft a preamble and resolutions for the consideration of a meeting of Bexar citizens and Alamo soldiers. Again, he is referred to as Colonel Bonham. The seventh resolution of the document that was passed in support of Gov. Henry Smith and Houston was a request that the entire document be published by the *Brazoria Gazette*, *Nacogdoches Telegraph*, and *San Felipe Telegraph*.[9]

On February 1, 1836, an election was held at the Alamo for the selection of two delegates to the coming Constitutional Convention. Bonham was nominated and received one vote from a soldier named P. H. Nash out of 103 cast.[10] The vote was taken in the form of an Australian ballot. The name of each voter was written down with the name of the person he voted for. As Bonham's name does not appear on the ballot as a voter and the fact that he received only one vote indicates he was not in the Alamo on election day. In all probability, Nash not only provided Bonham's lone vote but also cast his hat into the ring. Surely, had Bonham been in the Alamo, he would have received more than one vote.

Another bit of evidence that Bonham was gone from the Alamo is Colonel J. C. Neill's letter of February 5, 1836, to the convention in which he gave details of the election.[11] Besides Neill's signature, the letter was signed by R. White, Wm. A. Irwin, G. B. Jameson, E. Melton, Almeron Dickinson, W. H. Patton, Wm. B. Carey, W.C.W. Baker, Sam[ue]l Blair, Geo. Evans, Wm. Blazeby, W. Barret Travis and James Bowie. If Bonham was at the Alamo between February the first and the fifth, why did he fail to vote and why did he not sign Neill's letter to the convention? If Bonham was not at the Alamo during that time, where was he?

While there is no conclusive evidence to prove it, it seems logical that Bonham, as chairman of the committee, would have delivered the group's document to Governor Smith, the council and the three newspapers. As the document was surely a delight to Smith and Houston, it does not make sense that Bonham would have allowed another soldier to carry the good news to the east when there were probable political awards to garner from Smith and Houston. Also, the trip would have given Bonham a chance to check in on his law practice.

On February 16, Travis dispatched Bonham to Goliad to convince Colonel James W. Fannin, Jr., the acting commander-in-chief of the Texian military forces, to move his command to the Alamo.[12] In considering that trip and Bonham's other movements from February 16 to March 6, 1836, it is important to remember that when he left the Alamo on February 16, the Mexican army had not yet arrived. Travis, while concerned about getting the Alamo primed for a fight, was not expecting the Mexican forces to arrive until mid-March.[13]

Amelia Williams, Walter Lord and Lon Tinkle are a few of the historians who claim Bonham returned to the Alamo on February 23 with Fannin's refusal to send help. This belief that Bonham returned on the 23rd is undoubtedly based on only one piece of evidence. Dr. John Sutherland wrote that Bonham was outside the Alamo prospecting on land when the Mexican army arrived and returned to the Alamo, and he heard cannon fire at the mission.[14] Sutherland was wrong about Bonham's return for several reasons. First, Sutherland was not in the Alamo when he alleged Bonham returned. Second, Sutherland did not claim he saw or encountered Bonham outside of the Alamo on February 23. Thus, the good doctor must have obtained the information from another person who was in the Alamo on the 23rd and later left to survive the March 6 assault. If that was the case, Sutherland's information must have confused Bonham with someone else who returned to the Alamo on or about February 23.

Alamo defender David P. Cummings and ten other men left the mission-fortress on or about February 16 to prospect for land on the Cibolo River.[15] As Indian attacks were a common occurrence during those days, most individuals did not ride alone if there was a group to travel with. Thus, Bonham may have left Goliad with another Cummings group. Such an action on Bonham's part might explain why Sutherland thought Bonham was out of the Alamo searching for land.

In October of 1987, this writer pulled a document from the catacombs of Texas history that shows Bonham left the Alamo on February 16, and did not return until 11 A.M. on March 3. The document is a Spanish translation of a letter from Maj. R. M. Williamson to Col. William B. Travis.[16] Robert McAlpin "Three Legged Willie" Williamson was the commanding officer of the Texian ranging companies that were organized in the fall of 1835 to protect the settlements from Indian attacks, while the regular army and volunteer units fought the Mexicans.[17] Also, he was a lawyer, judge, poet and drinking buddy to Travis, his good friend.[18] The original Williamson letter was taken from Travis' body after the fall of the Alamo, and a Spanish translation of the letter appeared in a Mexican broadside on March 31, 1836.

Translated in English, the Williamson letter, addressed to Travis and dated March 1, 1836 (from Gonzales), is a moving document:

> You cannot conceive my anxiety: today it has been four whole days that we have not the slightest news relative to your dangerous situation and we are therefore given over to a thousand

conjectures regarding you. Sixty men have left this municipality, who in all probability are with you by this date. Colonel Fannin with 300 men and four pieces of artillery has been on the march towards Bexar three days now. Tonight we await some 300 reinforcements from Washington, Bastrop, Brazoria, and S. Felipe and no time will be lost in providing you assistance. As to the *other letter of the same date, let it pass*, you will know what it meant: if the multitude gets hold of it, let them figure it out.

> Your true friend
> R. M. Williamson

P.S. For God's sake hold out until we can assist you. I remit to you with major Bonham a communication from the interim governor. Best wishes to all your people and tell them to hold on firmly by their "wills" until I go there.
> Williamson

Write us very soon.

    The information within the Williamson letter proves the two translations to be valid. Williamson was the officer in charge at Gonzales. Fannin did leave for the Alamo with 300 men and four cannon. Not counting John W. Smith, Sutherland, and Juan Seguin, Alamo messengers who organized groups to reinforce Travis, sixty men had left Gonzales for the Alamo as of March 1, 1836.[19] If the Sutherland and Sequin groups had not stopped on the Cibolo River ford on the Bexar-Goliad road to wait for Fannin's troops, they would have been within the walls of the Alamo or perhaps dead in the ditch when Williamson wrote the letter.[20]

    Without doing a complete analysis of the letter's impact on Alamo history, what does it show us about Bonham's involvement in the Alamo defense? Probably the most important revelation is that Williamson believed Fannin had been on the road three days to reinforce the Alamo. The information contradicts the current belief that Bonham rode to the Alamo to inform Travis that Fannin was not coming. Next, the letter shows that Juan Seguin who left the Alamo on the night of February 25 with a message for Sam Houston, was the last messenger from the Alamo to ride to Gonzales as of March 1, 1836.[21]

Amelia Williams wrote that Bonham left the Alamo on February 27 for a second trip to Goliad.[22] If that was really the case, he would have probably arrived at Goliad on either the 28th or 29th, and would have learned of Fannin's departure to the Alamo, the subsequent breakdown of equipment on the east side of the San Antonio River, and the council of war that resulted in Fannin returning to his "Fort Defiance." The fact that the Williamson letter says Fannin was on his way to the Alamo, and the fact Bonham carried the letter into the Alamo shows that Bonham had not been at Goliad after February 27; otherwise, he would have known Fannin was staying put at Goliad.

Where did Bonham go after talking to Fannin on or about February 18? To answer that question it is necessary to go a little deeper into the reason Bonham went to Goliad in the first place. Alamo historians, to the last one, agree he rode to Goliad to obtain reinforcements for the Alamo. This writer does not believe Bonham's mission was that simple. Travis not only wanted Fannin's troops, he wanted Fannin to take command of the Alamo. Unbelievable, you shout! Individuals who believe Travis wanted to command at the Alamo have chosen to accept the mythical Travis created by Texas historians, rather than accept the words of the real Travis. The man did not even want to go the Alamo!

On January 29, Travis wrote Gov. Henry Smith from Burnham's on the Colorado River.[23] He requested the order sending him to the Alamo to be be recalled. Then he wrote the following: "I am willing, nay anxious, to go to the defense of Bexar, but, sir, I am unwilling to risk my reputation (which is ever dear to a soldier) by going off into the enemy's country with such little means, so few men, and with them so badly equipped. In fact, there is no necessity for my services to command these men."

Could anybody really blame Travis for not wanting to go to the Alamo? It was hardship duty. Dr. James Grant and his men had stripped the mission-fortress of its cannon, supplies and clothing for their idiotic Matamoros expedition. The Council seemed content to ignore that the Alamo troops were dressed in rags instead of uniforms and had not been paid in many a day. Sam Houston wanted the place abandoned and blown up as it did not fit in his defense plans for Texas. True, the local Mexican girls were pretty, but Travis had plenty of sweethearts around San Felipe. Also, his young son had only recently arrived in Texas. However, true to his nature, Travis did what only the best soldiers do when unable to get an assignment changed: he put his entire being into doing the best job possible.

Around February 12, Colonel Neill, the commanding officer at the Alamo, had to leave due to a sickness in his family. As Travis was the next senior army officer, Neill "volunteered" him to take command of the Alamo. Within hours of the appointment, James Bowie squared off with Travis over who would actually give the orders at the Alamo. On February 13, Travis wrote Gov. Henry Smith and informed him of the problems he had with Bowie.[24] He wrote: "If you had taken the trouble to answer my letter from Burnham's, I should not now have been under the necessity of troubling you." It appears Travis was referring to his letter of January 29, 1836, in which he asked Smith to recall the order sending him to the Alamo. Travis went on to write the following: "I do not solicit the command of this post but as Col [.] Neill (who) has applied to the Commander in Chief to be relieved is anxious for me to take command, I will do it if it be your order for a time until an artillery officer can be sent here."

Perhaps Travis, as a cavalry officer and one who realized that the coming battle would be an artillery clash, did not feel qualified to command the Alamo. The previous December when Travis heard the council was about to commission him a major in the artillery, he wrote James W. Robinson and asked that the commission be given to Francis W. Johnson.[25] Travis stated that he felt he could be more useful elsewhere in the Texas military. In early December, he had written the council a letter in which he had detailed the advantages of organizing a cavalry battalion under the command of a lieutenant colonel who would answer only to the commander-in-chief.[26] Clearly, "Buck" Travis felt that if he had to die in defense of Texas, it should be with saber and shotgun in his hands, astride a fast horse. Or, perhaps Travis was worn out—too beat to fight with the "living legend" Jim Bowie. Whatever Travis' reasons, he specified he be replaced with an artillery officer. In closing the letter, Travis wrote: "In conclusion allow me to beg that you will give me definite orders immediately."

On arriving at Goliad on or about February 18, Bonham probably received a conditional answer from Fannin with regard to moving the Goliad troops to the Alamo. While there is no evidence of exactly what Fannin told Bonham, on February 16, Fannin wrote Acting Gov. James W. Robinson and the council a letter in which he stated he would go to Bexar under certain conditions.[27]

The relevant part of the letter reads: "If General Houston does not return to duty on the expiration of his furlough, and it meets your approbation, I shall make headquarters at Bexar, and take with me such of the force as can be spared. I hope to have this place well secured by the time I can hear from you. If I do not go to Bexar, I would prefer the reserve army, and think I could do some service. In this, do with me, while a public servant, as you deem best. Bexar and Guadalupe, and Colorado, I think will be the posts of danger and honour."

One piece of evidence shows that Bonham, after having talked with Fannin, must have traveled northeast to see either Gov. Henry Smith or Houston. In 1838, Bonham's brother, Milledge, came to Texas to settle Bonham's affairs. At that time, Milledge Bonham discussed his brother's Alamo experiences with Houston. According to Milledge, Houston told him that he (Houston) "requested Colonel Bonham, on his leaving for San Antonio to urge Colonel Travis, commanding at the Alamo to fall back and unite his forces with the main army to more successfully defend the country against the invaders."[28]

The content of Houston's statement to Milledge Bonham shows that the Houston-James Bonham conversation had to have taken place after Travis had assumed command of the Alamo and after the Mexicans had arrived at Bexar. Historians have always considered the Milledge Bonham evidence as invalid because they believed Bonham was either at the Alamo or on the road to Goliad and Gonzales while Houston was in East Texas during the time period indicated by the Houston statement. As the Williamson letter shows, Bonham did not return to the Alamo after the February 16 trip, and that a second trip was not made, the Milledge Bonham evidence now appears to be valid.

Why did Bonham travel to the Texian colonies after leaving Goliad? Unless a trip to the area was already in his plans when he left the Alamo, Bonham probably decided to visit there after failing to convince Fannin to relocate to the Alamo. As a special messenger, Bonham may have gone to see Gov. Henry Smith to obtain an answer about an artillery officer who could relieve Travis, a concern of Travis' that was rendered null and void when the Mexican army caught the Bexar garrison and the entire country unprepared for a fight. At that time, Bowie and Travis buried the hatchet—or perhaps it was Bowie's knife—and agreed to work together against the Mexicans. Later, when Bowie fell ill, the command became Travis' total responsibility.

On the other hand, since the Mexicans were not expected until mid-March, Bonham may have been prospecting for land while on his way to the March 1 convention, and visiting Fannin for Travis was nothing more than a side trip. It seems logical that Bonham would have wanted to attend the convention as it would have given him the opportunity to meet many prominent Texians. In sum, there is no way to know for sure why Bonham went to the colonial areas of Texas after talking with Fannin, unless new evidence is someday located to furnish an answer.

When did Bonham talk to Houston? Again, this is a question for which history appears to hold no exact answer. On February 23, when the Mexican Army entered Bexar, Houston was at Chief Bowles' Cherokee village, where a treaty between the Cherokee and other tribes was completed with the Provisional Government of Texas.[29] Then, on February 26, word of the Alamo situation reached Acting Gov. James W. Robinson at Washington-on-the-Brazos. Robinson sent a message to Houston explaining the situation and requesting Houston to return to headquarters.[30] The letter was addressed to "Where-ever he may be. Send this by express day & night." It is not known if the express reached Houston, but the general arrived at Washington-on-the-Brazos on February 29 to represent Refugio as a delegate in the convention. His entry created quite a bit of excitement as he ignored Robinson and reported to his governor and friend, Henry Smith.[31]

It will probably be impossible to ever determine the exact date on which Houston talked to Bonham, but it most likely took place between February 27 and 29. It may have been that Bonham joined Houston at Chief Bowles' village and learned of the Alamo situation when Houston was informed. One thing is for sure: Bonham's presence at Gonzales on March 1, 1836, indicates that if the conversation with Houston took place on February 29, after Houston entered Washington-on-the-Brazos, Bonham must have had a hell-bent-for-leather ride to Gonzales.

Written records show that Houston, Travis and J. C. Neill referred to Bonham as "Colonel Bonham" even though his actual Texas rank was lieutenant. That being the case, why on March 1, 1836, at Gonzales did Williamson refer to Bonham as "major Bhanham[sic]?" While at Washington-on-the-Brazos did he receive some kind of special promotion that would allow him to command the artillerymen of the Alamo? It is obvious from Travis' letters he either did not want to or did not feel qualified to command an artillery battle; however, Bonham had been a colonel of artillery in South Carolina. Thus, on February 16, did Travis instruct Bonham that on failing to convince Fannin to move to the Alamo, he (Bonham) should travel to Henry Smith, or to Robinson and the council, and obtain a promotion to major of artillery? As it appears everybody with any authority called Bonham "Colonel." It does not seem logical that Williamson would have referred to him as "major," unless that was the rank Bonham held on that date.

The evidence shows that Bonham entered the Alamo on March 3, 1836, with at least three messages for Travis. The word from Williamson, Travis' good friend, was to "hold on" until help arrived from Gonzales, Goliad and other Texian settlements. Houston's message was to "fall back" and join the main army, an action that was impossible on March 3. Had the Alamo troops attempted to escape the fortress in mass, they probably would have died on the sharp points of Mexican cavalry lances without costing Santa Anna too many men. The third message was from the "interim governor," which was probably acting Governor Robinson but its content is unknown.

A few of the old questions about James Butler Bonham's

Texas experience have been given new answers in this article, and a body of new questions is left to roast on history's campfire for Alamo zealots to feast upon with their Bowie knives. Yet, one more question remains for this writer to answer before closing: Who, if anyone, urged Bonham to retreat from entering the Alamo on March 3? Amelia Williams, to her credit, presented evidence that showed Samuel A. Maverick and John W. Smith were not with Bonham on the morning of March 3. Smith was already at the Alamo, having guided the Gonzales and Chenoweth men into the Alamo on the morning of March 1. Maverick, an Alamo delegate to the convention, was at Washington-on-the-Brazos. However, Williams only replaced Brown's incident of the fictional history with one of her own design.[32]

Sometime after the Alamo siege started, Travis sent Benjamin Highsmith to Goliad with a message for Fannin to blow up the presidio and hurry to the Alamo. The round-trip took five days. When Highsmith returned to the Alamo, he found it surrounded by Mexican cavalry.[33] Amelia Williams claimed Highsmith was the person who urged Bonham not to enter the Alamo as it was sure death. As a source to support her claim, Williams said she used information from page nine of A. J. Sowell's *Early Settlers and Indian Fighters*. Her footnote reads: "A. J. Sowell states that Travis sent Ben Highsmith to Goliad with a message to Fannin, and that on his return 'on or about March 3,' he found the Alamo closely invested. The Mexican cavalry on the lookout for Texan couriers, chased him and his companion and they returned to Gonzales."

A careful reading of page nine of Sowell's book shows two points of conflict with Williams' reading of the page.[34] The page says nothing about Highsmith returning "on or about March 3." Second, Sowell did not write anything about Highsmith having a companion on his return to the Alamo. The relevant part of page nine reads: "The daring messenger saw there was no chance for him to communicate with his gallant commander, and slowly rode north towards the San Antonio and Gonzales road. The Mexican cavalrymen saw him, and a dense body of them rode parallel with and closely watched him. Finally they spurred their horses into a gallop and came rapidly towards him. Highsmith took one last look towards the Alamo and the trapped heroes within, and then turning his horse east, dashed off towards Gonzales."

It is also interesting to note that the Bonham entry scene John Henry Brown staged in his story for *Farm and Ranch* does not appear in his *History of Texas*.[35] In the history book, Brown stuck to the known facts of Bonham's return as described by Travis' letter of March 3.[36] As for the white handkerchief and the cream-white horse Brown attributed to Bonham, they appear to be Brown's way of tagging some post Civil War symbolism to Bonham's heroic return to the Alamo.

If anyone urged Bonham not to return to the Alamo, it was either Houston or Williamson. Both men were in a position to have done so, and both would have had a good reason. Also, both men were dead by the time historians became interested in the exact nature of Bonham's return to the Alamo, which could explain why either man's story could have been lost to history.

Sam Houston clearly liked James Butler Bonham, and if anyone realized there was not enough time to group and equip a sufficient army to save the Alamo, it was the "Raven." Texas had been caught unprepared and Houston probably saw that the Alamo would only be part of the price Texas would have to pay before a final victory. Thus, it seems reasonable to believe that Houston would have urged Bonham to stay in East Texas.

On March 1 or 2, when Bonham left Gonzales for the Alamo, the people of Gonzales had not heard from Travis for at least four days. For all they knew, the Alamo defenders were dead, and Fannin was fighting Santa Anna someplace off the Goliad-Bexar road. Thus Bonham rode west from Gonzales, not knowing what awaited him at the Alamo. It is possible Williamson may have urged him to remain at Gonzales until fresh news arrived from Travis.

While James Butler Bonham could never have been a "Man of Steel," two facts are diamond clear about him: his courage and honor were as strong and sharp as the Damascus blade of Jim Bowie's big butcher knife, and his place behind Crockett, Bowie and Travis was rightfully earned on that March morning in 1836 when he returned to the Alamo.

Notes

1. Seth Shepard, *The Fall of the Alamo*. A paper read at a meeting of the San Marcos Chautauqua Assembly, July 8, 1889, at San Marcos, Texas, 15-16.
2. Amelia Williams, "A Critical Study of the Siege of the Alamo and of the Personnel of Its Defenders," *The Southwest Historical Quarterly*, Vol. XXXVII (July 1933 to April 1934), 25.
3. Walter Lord, *A Time to Stand* (London: Longmans, Green and Co. Ltd., 1962), 135.
4. James B. Bonham to Sam Houston, Dec. 1, 1835, The A. J. Houston Collection, Archives, Texas State Library, Austin.
5. Williams, 248. Williams' sources for Bonham's rank were his military pay record, which can be found in the Audited Military Claims Collection of the Archives of the Texas State Library, and a letter from Bonham to Houston dated Dec. 31, 1835, which is missing from the Archives of the Texas State Library. Either the letter is misplaced among the thousands of documents or it was taken in years past when the library's security was not as good as it is today.
6. Lon Tinkle, *13 Days to Glory* (New York: McGraw-Hill, 1958), 147.
7. *Ibid.*
8. Dr. John Sutherland, *The Fall of the Alamo* (San Antonio: The Naylor Company, 1936), 22-23.
9. San Antonio Meeting, John H. Jenkins, ed., *The Papers of the Texas Revolution 1835-1836*, Vol. IV (Austin: Presidial Press, 1973), 153-155.
10. Alamo Election Return for Delegates to Constitutional Convention of 1836, Archives, Texas State Library. This important document was found by Texas' Kevin Young.
11. Neill, et. al., to Convention, Jenkins, 263-265.
12. Travis to Convention, Jenkins, 502-504.
13. Travis to Smith, Jenkins, 327-328.
14. Sutherland, 22-23.
15. Cummings to Cummings, Jenkins, 333-335.
16. Williamson to Travis, Jenkins 485. Williamson's letter was taken from Travis' body after the fall of the Alamo. A Spanish translation of the letter appeared in an account of the battle in a Mexican broadside on March 31, 1836. For this article, the Spanish version of the letter was translated to English by Mr. Jesus de la Teja, assistant archivist for the Archives and Records Division of the Texas General Land Office.
17. Houston to Williamson, Jenkins, Vol. III, 259-260. Houston instructed Williamson to set up Ranger recruiting headquarters at Mina (Bastrop); Williamson to Governor and Council, Jenkins, Vol. IV, 434-435.
18. Tinkle, 95.
19. Sutherland, 27. On February 27, 1836, twenty-five men left Gonzales with John W. Smith acting as their guide. On Sunday, February 28, Sutherland left Gonzales with Dr. Horace Alsbury and ten Americans. After crossing the Guadalupe River at Gonzales, they joined Juan Seguin who had rounded up twenty-four men to return to the Alamo.
20. *Ibid.*

21. Travis to Houston, Jenkins, Vol. IV, 433-434.
22. Williams, 307.
23. Travis to Smith, Jenkins, 185.
24. Travis to Smith, Jenkins, 327-328
25. Travis to Robinson, Jenkins, Vol. III, 241-242.
26. Travis to Council, Jenkins, 91-93.
27. Fannin to Robinson, Jenkins, Vol. IV, 350-351.
28. Milledge L. Bonham, Jr., "James Butler Bonham: A Consistent Rebel," *The Southwestern Historical Quarterly*, Vol. XXXV (July 1931 to April 1932), 129. The articles's footnote shows the Sam Houston–James B. Bonham conversation evidence came from a memorandum on the life of J. B. Bonham, in the papers of Milledge Luke Bonham, which in 1931 were in the possession of Milledge L. Bonham, Jr., the article's author.
29. Houston, et. al, Treaty, Jenkins, 415-418.
30. Robinson to Houston, Jenkins, 445.
31. Donald Braider, *Solitary Star* (New York: G. P. Putnam's Sons, 1974), 147.
32. Williams, 26.
33. A. J. Sowell, *Early Settlers and Indian Fighters of Southwest Texas* (New York: Argosy-Antiquarian Ltd., 1964), 9.
34. *Ibid.*
35. John Henry Brown, *History of Texas*, Vol. I (St. Louis: L. E. Daniell, 1892), 565.
36. Travis to Convention, Jenkins, 502-504. In November 1835, a provisional government consisting of a governor, lieutenant governor, and council was created to run the country. Henry Smith became the governor and James W. Robinson took the position of lieutenant governor. In early January 1836, the council authorized Dr. James Grant and Col. Frank Johnson to capture Matamoros, Mexico. However, Johnson dropped out of the foolish plan. As a result, the council appointed James Fannin as its agent to replace Johnson. A few days later, Johnson changed his mind and took up the Matamoros cause again. Thus, counting Houston, Texas had four supreme military commanders. All of the council's acts had been implemented over Governor Smith's veto. Smith issued a statement denouncing the acts and the council. The council responded by impeaching Smith and promoting Robinson to the position of acting governor. As the council had no power to impeach him, Smith refused to give up the Texas archives and state seal. His other answer to the Council was that he would shoot "any son of a bitch" who tried to take the archives and state seal away from him. Houston and the men of the Alamo stood with Smith, while Fannin sided with Robinson and the council. According to Sutherland, seven of the Gonzales thirty-two were picked up at the Cibolo River crossing on the Bexar-Goliad Road. The men came from Captain Chenoweth's company of mounted volunteers called the "United States Invincibles," which were part of Fannin's Goliad command. A total of nine men from Chenoweth's company died at the Alamo. Since four of the men were already in the Alamo on February 1, 1836, when they voted in the election of convention delegates, it may be that only five men joined the Gonzales group.

ABOUT THE ARTICLE'S AUTHOR

Thomas Ricks Lindley

Thomas Ricks Lindley is a Texas-based historical researcher, and the author of *Alamo Traces: New Evidence and New Conclusions*.

Over the years he was written many important articles for The Alamo Journal, including "Alamo Sources" (issue no. 74; Feb. 1991), "Alamo Artillery: Number, Type, Caliber and Concussion" (no. 82; July 1992), "A Correct List of Alamo Patriots" (no. 89; Dec. 1993) and "James Butler Bonham, October 17, 1835-March 6, 1836" (no. 62; August 1988), which is included in this book.

Lindley and fellow Alamo Society member, Dr. James E. Crisp, participated in a spirited debate over the death of David Crockett and the legitimacy of the José Enrique de la Peña papers in several issues. Lindley contributed "Killing Crockett: It's All in the Execution" (no. 96; May 1995), "Killing Crockett (part 2): Theory Paraded as Fact" (no. 97 July 1995) and "Killing Crockett: Lindley's Opinion (no. 98; Oct. 1995)."

Lindley later wrote "José Enrique de la Peña's Petard" (no. 107; Dec. 1997), "The Prima Facie Evidence That De La Peña is a Forgery" (no. 113; June 1999), and "At the Alamo Walls Again" (no. 119; 2000).

Lindley created the "Documents of the Texian Revolution" section in *The Alamo Journal*, and has contributed many documents to that department. He has also provided research assistance to several authors who have published works on the Alamo and the Texas Revolution.

He was featured in the December 1993 issue of *Texas Monthly*. Writer Gregory Curtis remarked about Lindley's research efforts: "His work does not depend on the findings of dowsers or the visions of a mystic but on hours upon hours of what he calls 'hard chair time' in the [Texas State] archives and the General Land Office."

ABOUT THE ARTIST

John Bourdage

John Bourdage is a freelance artist and actor who has been involved in various creative and living-history activities for several decades. He composed his first cover for *The Alamo Journal* in October 1988 (no. 63). Since then, he has illustrated *Alamo Journal* covers for May (no. 66), August (no. 67), and December (no. 69) of 1989, December 1990 (no. 74), February (no. 75), and December 1991 (no. 79), and May of 1993 (no. 86).

In addition, Bourdage has created numerous illustrations—from battle scenes and weapons to portraits and cartoons—for the pages of *The Alamo Journal*, as well as artistic creations for such organizations as the Little Big Horn Associates, and the Custer Battlefield Historical and Museum Association.

His artwork stems from his extensive, living-history experiences, which originated in 1972 at a mountain man rendezvous at the Cascades Mountains in Washington State.

A competitive shooter in the North-South Skirmish Association in the 1970s, Bourdage later participated as a trooper in the recreated 7th Cavalry living-history organization at the Little Big Horn battlesite in Montana. Following the Texas Sesquicentennial in 1986, he participated in various living-history events in the Lone Star State, from San Antonio to San Jacinto.

He has been seen in such film productions as *Gambler 5* with Kenny Rogers, *James A. Michener's Texas* with Stacy Keach, the television series *Heaven Help Us* with John Schneider, and *Under One Roof* with James Earl Jones.

"North Wall Diggers Under Fire" by Gary Zaboly, Alamo Journal, no. 101 (June 1996).

Manning The Walls

Robert L. Durham

Countless books and magazine articles have described the final assault on the Alamo, but none have accounted for the distribution of the defenders along the walls of the mission–fortress. Much study has gone into finding the number of total defenders, even down to the name of each individual, and it is fairly certain how many Mexican soldiers were in each attacking column. However, no endeavor to reconstruct the final moments in the siege can be accurate without also trying to reconstruct approximately how many defenders were present along the stretch of wall that each offensive column was assaulting.

To be able to evaluate the dynamics of the final assault, one needs to know what each attacking column faced as it approached the Alamo. How much musket and cannon fire did they brave before they reached the walls? What did the Mexican soldiers confront in the way of hand-to-hand weapons when they came in close quarters with the rebels? While no documentation exists to fairly assess this problem, a little creative logic should provide a fairly accurate estimate.

As a starting point, the estimated number of total defenders is at least 189. Also, the Alamo featured some twenty-one cannon, sixteen of which would have had assigned crews.[1] Of the other five, the Alamo defenders positioned two guns on a platform in the plaza facing the main gate. These unmanned weapons, which may not even have had gun carriages, were meant to fire a parting shot into any enemy rushing through the main gate.[2] Three cannon, probably the smallest pieces, were unused.

Due to the manpower shortage, the defenders could not have assigned a full crew. Some ten to fifteen men, including matrosses, served a field gun on the march. Two men could conceivably operate a cannon but a five-man crew is more realistic.[3] Therefore, the cannoneers for the sixteen artillery pieces account for eighty men, leaving 109. Jim Bowie was ill and at least two men (James McGee and James Nowlan) who were seriously injured in the Battle for Bexar were probably still in the compound's hospital during the battle.[4] That allows for some 106 men present for duty during the thirteen-day siege. There were four doctors (Amos Pollard, William Howell, Edward Mitchasson and John Thomson) assigned to the medical staff of the fortress, leaving 102 officers and men serving as infantrymen.[5]

Popular conception would have some of us believe that all of the Alamo defenders were frontiersmen, deadly marksmen armed with long rifles. That was not the case. Most were farmers and tradesmen armed with smooth-bore muskets and shotguns. One advantage that the defenders had over the attackers was the number of weapons available to each individual. The rebels captured many Brown Bess muskets when they took Bexar in December of 1835. As a result, there would have been enough to supply every defender with several weapons.

When it comes to assessing the hand-to-hand weapons available to the Texians, myth comes into play again. The image of burly, buckskin-clad bravos armed with clubbed rifles, Bowie knives, tomahawks and fists locked in close combat with bayonet and sword-wielding attackers is a hard one to dismiss. However, among the muskets captured at Bexar were bayonets and swords. The Texians, no doubt, used many of these confiscated weapons—and Mexican accounts stated that they did.

The Church

The defenses of the Alamo had several distinct areas. The church, for example, featured a gun ramp that was built from the eastern wall of the structure. It was fortified with three of the garrison's larger pieces and was manned by fifteen artillerists. In addition to the cannoneers, there were four officers: Maj. Robert Evans (ordnance officer), Lt. Eliel Melton (quartermaster), Lt. Almeron Dickinson (battery commander) and 2nd Lt. James Butler Bonham.

The church walls, too high to be scaled, had no need for a large number of riflemen. However, there were probably at least two men stationed on the church's walls next to the Long Barracks. In addition, Susanna Dickinson, who was sheltered in the southwest room of the church during the storming of the Alamo, later stated that besides Juan Melton[6] and Anthony Wolf's two children, defenders Jacob Walker and Galba Fuqua were also in the room.[7] Thus, some twenty-three men were stationed in the church.

During the attack, the Texians directed two of the cannon against the troops under Francisco Duque who were assaulting the east walls of the convent yard. The artillery's impact helped force Duque's column to veer to the north. The third cannon helped break up the attack against the palisade by the troops under Col. Juan Morales. The gunners in the church may have directed their fire on the approximate 385 Mexican cavalry under Gen. Agustin Amat, who were picketing to the south and east of the Alamo.[8]

After the Mexicans gained entry to the Alamo grounds, the last stronghold they assailed was the church. The attackers blasted down the building's massive front doors with one of the Alamo's artillery pieces. The high front wall of the church prevented the platform-mounted guns from being fired against the advancing troops in the courtyard; however, the defenders probably turned one of the guns on the first soldiers who rushed through the destroyed front doors.

Once the Mexican soldiers gained entrance to the church, it probably did not take long to eliminate the few remaining defenders. Lt. Melton leaped from the church wall, clutching a bundle that several Mexican soldiers mistakenly thought was a child.[9] The cavalry pickets outside shot and killed him when he reached the ground. The Mexican infantrymen who assaulted the church shot Major Evans as he tried to reach the powder magazine with a lighted torch. Jacob Walker was bayoneted near Susanna Dickinson who remained in the baptistry just to the right of the church's main entrance. The enraged Mexican soldiers also bayoneted both of Anthony Wolf's young sons.

The Palisade

Some fourteen riflemen of the Tennessee Mounted Volunteers under the command of Capt. William B. Harrison defended one of the weakest points of the fortification: the palisade, a section of the Alamo compound that extended from the church to the eastern end of the South Wall.[10] In addition, a gun crew of five manned the artillery piece in the center of the palisade.[11] Thus, at least nineteen Texians were stationed at the palisade.

The palisade was the original objective of the south assault column of light infantry, approximately 105 men under Morales. The concentrated fire of the Tennesseans and other defenders along the South Wall forced the Mexicans to shift westward. Morales' men, utilizing the cover provided by some of the structures located southwest of the Alamo, renewed their attack against the southwest corner of the garrison. Perhaps some of the palisade defenders, possibly under Crockett, moved over the southern portion of the West Wall to lend assistance. It is at this location that Francisco Ruiz found the body of Crockett after the battle.[12] The remaining Tennesseans and artillerymen may have attempted to defend the palisade area when the Mexican assault columns gained entrance to the large courtyard. However, it is more likely that the Texians retreated into the Long Barracks or the church.

Subtracting the fourteen Tennessee Mounted Volunteer riflemen from the number of total defenders left the Alamo with eighty-five infantrymen to guard the remainder of the mission–fortress' walls. Approximately 480 yards of wall surrounded the Alamo. When one subtracts 83 yards from that total for various cannon platforms, 397 yards remained for the rest of the riflemen to defend. Dividing the number of yards of wall by the number of riflemen yields 4.67 yards of wall per man.

The South Wall

The South Wall, after subtracting the space taken for the gun platform at the southwest corner, was approximately 58 yards long. An estimated twelve riflemen (58 divided by 4.67) were assigned to protect the Low Barracks and main gate. The defenders had two cannon mounted behind the fosse protecting the gate. A small three-pounder in a room east of the gate and an eighteen-pounder on the platform in the southwest corner added to the firepower on this wall.[13] Five men per gun adds up to twenty artillerists.

The 105 infantrymen under Colonel Morales assailing the Alamo from the south, faced approximately fifty-eight defenders and six cannon, not quite a two-to-one advantage. Being trained as light infantrymen, they probably advanced in skirmish order; therefore, they did not present the compact target of the advancing column. These soldados were all elite troops, armed with Baker rifles rather than smooth bore Brown Bess muskets.

The concentrated fire from the walls repelled the Mexican soldiers initially. Consequently, some of the troops occupied some dwellings, probably ruins at this stage of the siege, southwest of the Alamo. From the cover of these structures, they sniped at the defenders until the troops in the other attacking columns gained entrance to the main courtyard. With the attention of the garrison diverted by the troops storming the compound behind them, Morales' men successfully stormed the cannon platform at the southwest corner. Assaulted from front and rear, there were probably not many defenders stationed on the roof of the Low Barracks who were able to find safety within the rooms beneath them.

Contrary to some Alamo movies, the Mexican troops never did blow up and storm the main gate because there was no reason to. After gaining entrance to the compound by storming the walls, they assaulted the gate's defenders from behind. Some of these defenders, cut off from their companions inside the Alamo, probably leaped over the low barricade and tried to escape. One account suggests that a defender hid under a bridge over the San Antonio River until a woman washing clothes spotted him. She informed the Mexican soldiers who later seized and executed him.[14]

Among the individuals who manned the defense of the South Wall were Sgt. William B. Ward, who was stationed at one of the guns behind the fortifications protecting the main gate.[15] Ward may have been at this assignment during the final assault. Some of Juan Seguin's cavalry company manned the cannon mounted in the room of the Low Barracks east of the fosse. These men included José Gregorio Esparza and Toribio Loysoya.[16] The bodies of both men were found there after the battle—Esparza's with a bullet wound in his chest and a sword wound in his side.[17]

The old guardroom just west of the main gate was a refuge for many of the women and children in the Alamo. When the Mexican troops stormed the darkened room, they fired indiscriminately killing a paralyzed man and an unidentified young boy.[18] The soldiers also killed a Mexican trumpeter before he was able to identify himself; he had been captured in a sortie early in the siege. One of the South Wall's defenders, Brigido Guerrero, had sought sanctuary in the room with the noncombatants. He allegedly talked his way free by claiming that he had been a prisoner of the Texians.[19] Another occupant of one of the Low Barracks' rooms was Jim Bowie. Already near death, the legendary knife fighter was probably unable to put up much of a fight when Mexican soldiers smashed down the door to his room.[20]

The West Wall

The West Wall probably had a cannon platform at each end, and two guns along its length, which fired through window-cannon ports.[21] Subtracting the space taken by the cannon emplacements leaves approximately 145 yards of wall space, which was defended by thirty-one riflemen. Each of the gun crews required five men each.

The cannon situated just to the north of the eighteen-pounder was a twelve-pounder gunade, which was particularly lethal when firing canister at close range.[22] The defenders converted the southern half of the dry acequia that flowed through the plaza into a fortified trench, which created a small redoubt along the West Wall. The small fortification is where Alcalde Ruiz found Davy Crockett's body after the battle.[23]

The light infantry under Colonel Morales subjected the southern portion of the West Wall to a sniping attack from a position of cover. Later, Gen. Martin Perfecto de Cos' line of infantry attacked and scaled the northern position of the wall. At least part of the troops defending the West Wall may have rushed to lend aid to the Texians on the North Wall where the main Mexican attack had taken place. Therefore, the troops had gained entrance to the compound after assaulting from the north. Morales saw his chance and assailed the southwest gun platform.[24] When the Mexicans took the gun platform, the defenders in the small fortification along the West Wall were uncovered along their left flank. The troops flowing into the compound from the north and southwest corner prevented these defenders from retreating to the last ditch defenses in the Long Barracks. Most of these Texians, who were battered from all sides, died where they stood.

There were four buildings along the West Wall that contained six rooms. The southern-most room was the artillery command post. The next building to the north was the headquarters of the Alamo. Col. William Barret Travis and his slave, Joe, occupied one of the two rooms here. When the adjutant, Capt. John Baugh, gave the alarm that the Mexicans were attacking, Travis and Joe raced to the gun platform at the northwest corner. Upon the death of his master, Joe ran back to his room where he remained until the end of the battle.

Juana de Navarro Alsbury, her son, Alijo Perez, and her sister, Gertrudis de Navarro, utilized one of the other rooms along the West Wall. The two women were the adopted sisters of Jim Bowie's wife. When the Mexicans rushed the Alamo, Juana left the refuge of the room, hoping to show that only women and children were inside. One of the Texians, either Edwin T. Mitchell or Napoleon B. Mitchell, tried to protect her but the Mexicans butchered him. A Tejano defender, probably one of Seguin's men, sought cover behind her but a Mexican soldier killed him.[25] Except for looting their trunks, the Mexican soldiers did not harm Señora Alsbury or her sister.

The North Wall

The North Wall had three guns and fifteen artillerymen. One of the guns shared the platform on the northwest corner with the cannon defending the West Wall. The defenders deployed the other two cannons on a ramp in the center of the wall. Just to the east of this platform was a rough picket fence reinforced with earth that the Texians had constructed following damage caused by the Mexican artillery. Not counting the space taken up by the cannon emplacements there were about fifty-three yards of wall defended by eleven riflemen. In addition, Colonel Travis and Capt. John Baugh were stationed in this area.

The three columns of General Cos, Col. Francisco Duque and Col. José Romero, numbering some 1,180 men, converged against the three cannon and the twenty-eight Texians who vainly attempted to hold the rampart. Some of the men along the West Wall and atop the artillerymen's barracks north of the Long Barracks, some twenty-five to thirty men, probably rushed to their companions' defense.

Still, against odds of over twenty-to-one, the valiant Texian defenders held on. The gallant Travis fell early in the battle when a musket ball pierced his temple. Finally, Gen. Santa Anna sent in the reserves against this short section of the wall. These additional 385 Mexican soldiers included approximately 200 grenadiers, the pick of the army. Cos redirected his men against the northern section of the West Wall, which allowed him to outflank the defenders. At the same time, the other troops succeeded in scaling the rough palisade built to reinforce the breach that the Mexican artillery had blasted in the wall during the siege.

Adobe Dwellings

The adobe dwellings that connected the North Wall with the Long Barracks and served as the quarters for the Alamo's artillerists were weaker than the stone houses constructed against the South and West Walls. As a result, Alamo engineer Maj. Green B. Jameson reinforced the walls with pickets.[26] The length of this part of the East Wall was approximately fifty-three yards long. Probably eleven riflemen guarded this section, which featured no cannon positions. This wall was the objective of Colonel Romero's men. Aided by the crossfire from the courtyard behind the Long Barracks and the church, the Texians repelled this initial attack and forced Romero to veer to the right where he joined Cos and Duque in the storming of the North Wall. Many of the Texians probably moved to the assistance of their companions who were trying to hold that wall. When the tide of Mexicans assaulting the North Wall proved irresistible, most of the surviving defenders retreated into the Long Barracks.

Long Barracks and Rear Courtyard

Low stone walls, only six feet high, protected the courtyard area behind the Long Barracks. A dry moat protected the outside of these walls. A cannon mounted on a strong redoubt secured the northeast angle. The cattle pen and horse corral were also situated in this area. These corrals must have included an inner fence to keep the animals segregated from the men stationed at the walls.

Subtracting the cannon emplacement leaves about thirty yards on the North Wall and approximately fifty-eight yards of East Wall where six and eleven riflemen, respectively, were stationed. Added to the five cannoneers, the number of courtyard area defenders totaled twenty-two. A gun crew manning the three-pounder mounted to the roof of the two-story hospital, the southern-most structure of the Long Barracks, provided a secondary line of defense for the courtyard.[27]

It seems that the low walls surrounding the courtyard invited attack but this did not happen. Perhaps the Mexicans thought it might prove to be a death trap for any troops caught inside the yard since they would be subject to a crossfire from the Long Barracks and church. At any rate, the fire power from the defenders of this area was able to inflict considerable damage to the left flank of Colonel Romero's column, which forced the unit to shift its attack to the right—against the North Wall. When the Mexicans gained the interior of the Alamo compound, most of the courtyard defenders joined the last defense effort with the Long Barracks. A few, however, attempted to escape to the east where the waiting Mexican cavalry cut them down. The badly wounded Henry Warnell eluded these horsemen in the predawn darkness.

Notes

1. Thomas Ricks Lindley, "Alamo Artillery: Number, Type, Caliber and Concussion," *The Alamo Journal*, no. 82, July 1992, [3-10].
2. Jake Ivey, "South Gate and Its Defenses," Alamo Lore and Myth Organization newsletter, Dec. 1981, 3.
3. Albert A. Nofi, *The Alamo and the Texas War for Independence* (Conshohocken, PA: Combined Books, 1992), 103-106.
4. Bill Groneman, *Alamo Defenders* (Austin, TX: Eakin Press, 1990), 77-78, 87.
5. Phil Rosenthal, "Alamo Surgeons," *Alamo II*, Jan., 1981, 4; Groneman, 62, 80-81, 91-92, 112-113.
6. Timothy M. Matovina, ed., *The Alamo Remembered: Tejano Accounts and Perspectives* (Austin, TX: University of Texas Press, 1995), 68-69.
7. Susanna Dickinson does not identify him, but Anthony Wolf was probably one of the defenders in the church. His children were sheltered in the church and a clear pattern is shown where defenders were stationed near their families. For this same reason, it is probable that Asa Walker, Jacob's cousin, may also have been stationed within the church's walls.
8. Francisco Becerra, *A Mexican Sergeant's Recollections of the Alamo and San Jacinto* (Austin, TX; Jenkins Publishing Co., 1980), 22.
9. Marshall De Bruhl, *Sword of San Jacinto: A Life of Sam Houston* (New York, NY: Random House, 1993), 183-184; R. M. Potter, *The Fall of the Alamo: A Reminiscence of the Revolution of Texas* (Bryan, TX: Fuller Printing Co., 1979, reprint), 11. Sam Houston's letter to Fannin on March 6, 1836, relates this incident but the identified individual is Lieutenant Dickinson. Potter's account does the same. However, Susanna Dickinson said that a man named Milton jumped off the wall of the church during the height of the battle. Still, the Mexican troops saw someone jump from the chapel walls. This account appears too many times to be dismissed.
10. Dr. John Sutherland, *The Fall of the Alamo* (San Antonio, TX: The Naylor Co., 1936), 20; Phil Rosenthal, "Tennessee Mounted Volunteers" *Alamo II*, Jan. 1981, 3; Groneman, 7-9, 22, 24, 26-29, 50, 58, 77, 92-93, 106-107, 111-113, 119.
11. The maps of the Alamo drawn by José Juan Sanchez Navarro and Col. Ygnacio de Labastida both show one cannon mounted in the center of the pal-

isade. The map by Navarro also shows a cannon defending the gap in the low wall separating this area from the main courtyard and another in front of the church door. The defenders probably positioned the guns in these two locations so they could more easily wheel cannon into either place if necessary. The only source identifying four guns along the palisade is the map made by R. M. Potter.

12. Matovina, 44.

13. Ivey, "South Gate ..." 3; Matovina, 64.

14. Walter Lord, *A Time to Stand* (New York: Harper & Row, 1961), 161. See Gary Zaboly's cover art for issue no. 99 (Dec. 1995) of *The Alamo Journal*.

15. Ward was seen there by Nat Lewis, a local merchant.

16. See note #7. Losoya would have been stationed on the South Wall to be near his wife. The most logical place where he would have been stationed was with Esparza at one of the guns. There is a strong possibility that many of Bowie's men may have been assigned to the defense of the South Wall in order to be near their leader.

17. Matovina, 34.

18. *Ibid.*, 66

19. *Ibid.*, 66, 69-71, 83. Most accounts place the Tejano survivors in the church with Mrs. Dickinson. However, the accounts of Ms. Dickinson and Enrique Esparza have nothing in common. Perhaps the differences in their accounts reflect where they were positioned in the Alamo. Also, there is no reason to dismiss Enrique's account of the Mexican prisoner.

20. Sutherland, 40.

21. Ivey, "Southwest and Northwest Gun Emplacements," Alamo Lore and Myth Organization newsletter, Sept. 1981, 1-5.

22. C. J. Long, 1836: *The Alamo* (San Antonio, TX: Daughters of the Republic of Texas, Inc., 1981), 6-8.

23. Ruiz clearly stated that he discovered the body of Crockett "Toward the west and in the fort opposite the city." This conflicts with Susanna Dickinson's statements in which she stated that she saw Crockett's body in the area between the church and the Long Barracks. Ruiz was probably correct. A "fort" must have been interior defenses and the ditch from the acequia would have been a natural starting point from which to construct such defensive works.

24. Don Vicente Filisola, *Memoirs For the History of the War in Texas* (Austin, TX: Eakin Press, 1987), 177.

25. Matovina, 45-46.

26. Green B. Jameson's index to the Plat of the Alamo shows this block of buildings as "Soldiers quarters built up doby houses and picketed all around." This seems perfectly reasonable although no modern drawings or paintings depict this wood picket reinforcement to the walls.

27. The Mexicans captured the flag of the New Orleans Grays on the roof of the Long Barracks, so it is reasonable to suggest that some of the men manning this cannon were from the unit. If this was the case, the Grays may have been the troops assigned to the courtyard area. Apart from assigning certain men to areas allowing them to be near their families, there would have been an attempt to maintain unit cohesion.

ABOUT THE ARTICLE'S AUTHOR

Robert L. Durham

Robert L. Durham is an Ohio-based computer specialist in the Defense Logistics Agency. His avocation is historical writing—especially such topics as the Texas Revolution, the American West, and the Civil War.

He has penned several articles for *The Alamo Journal* over the years including "Manning the Walls" (issue no. 102; September 1996), which explored the defenses of the Alamo during the famous thirteen-day siege and battle in 1836. "I wrote 'Manning the Walls' because I felt this was a long neglected and overdue subject for discussion," said the author. "Since writing this article, the number of Texian defenders has been revised upwards by many historians, but I believe my article still provides a useful tool for any analysis of the final assault."

Durham also wrote "Where Did Davy Die?" (issue no. 104; March 1997), which contributed to the ongoing debate about the death of Davy Crockett at the Alamo. His most recent contribution to the official publication of The Alamo Society was "Latest From Texas," which appeared in issue no. 136 (March 2005).

He wrote "Flashing Sabers at Solomon's Fork for *Wild West* magazine (Feb. 2002) and "African Americans at the Alamo" for the highly regarded "Alamo de Parras" website. He has also posted historical articles on the "Civil War St. Louis" website.

Durham has contributed book reviews to such publications as *True West* magazine and *Muzzleloader*.

He serves on the Book Review Staff of *The Civil War News* and since 2000 has reviewed many titles about America's War Between the States.

The Assault of the Alamo

An Evaluation of Santa Anna
According to the Principles of War

by William R. Chemerka

At the conclusion of an heroic thirteen-day siege, the Alamo garrison fell to the forces of General Santa Anna during the predawn darkness of March 6, 1836. Later in the day, before the sun set on the gallant mission–fortress, the bodies of David Crockett, William Barret Travis, James Bowie, James Butler Bonham, and over 180 others burned in funeral pyres. Although Santa Anna considered his attack on the Alamo "a small affair," the assault resulted in considerable Mexican casualties. Travis had noted that any potential Mexican victory would be so costly that it would be "worse ... than a defeat" for Santa Anna and his regiments.

Still, Santa Anna's plan to defeat the Alamo garrison resulted in a clear victory. The outcome at San Jacinto on April 21, 1836, of course, would be quite different for the self-proclaimed Napoleon of the West.

How well did Santa Anna achieve his victory at the Alamo? An examination and application of the Principles of War provides a probable qualitative answer.

The Principles of War have been enumerated in various United States Army publications, particularly *Field Manuals 100 and 105*. To be sure, the nine principles reflect but one codification of military theory; as a matter of fact, the legendary Chinese leader Sun Tzu (circa 500 B.C.) identified and explained thirteen

"Battle of the Alamo" by Howard Bender, Alamo Journal, *no. 122 (September 2001)*.

The Assault of the Alamo 79

such martial principles. And centuries later, Napoleon cited 115 military maxims.

According to Maurice Matloff, who edited the 1969 volume *American Military History*, these Principles of War have been periodically revised and modified by the United States Army.[1] Matloff has pointed out that these principles are not equal in their impact, since conditions and variables can emphasize some elements and de-emphasize others. Furthermore, battlefield commanders must sometimes take calculated risks, which seemingly reject accepted dogma, in order to achieve short-term objectives.

And what about General Antonio Lopez de Santa Anna?

The following Principles of War are stated and explained (in italics) in their entirety. The evaluation of Santa Anna's efforts against the command of William Barret Travis in 1836 immediately follows each principle.

Objective

Every military operation must be directed towards a clearly defined, decisive and attainable objective. The ultimate military objective of war is the destruction of the enemy's armed forces and his will to fight. The objective of each operation must contribute to this ultimate objective. Each intermediate objective must be such that its attainment will most directly, quickly and economically contribute to the purpose of that operation. The selection of an objective is based upon consideration of the means available, the enemy and the areas of operations. Every commander must understand and clearly define his objective and consider each contemplated action in light thereof.

Santa Anna's effort to destroy a number of Texian revolutionaries via the Alamo campaign was put into effect by his siege against the mission–fortress, which commenced on February 23, 1836. A final assault against the Alamo was initiated on March 6. Obviously, the total destruction of the Alamo garrison reduced the size of Texian forces in the field at that moment. Santa Anna concisely identified his goals to his officers on March 5: "The Permanent Battalion of Aldama (except the company of grenadiers) and the three right centre companies of the Active Battalion of San Luis, will compose the first column.

The second column will be commanded by Col. Don Francisco Duque, and in his absence, by Gen. Don Manuel Fernandez Castrillon: it will be composed of the Active Battalion of Toluca (except the company of Grenadiers) and the three remaining centre companies of the active Battalion of San Luis.

The third column will be commanded by Col. José Maruia Romero, and in his absence, by Col. Mariano Salas; it will be composed of the Permanent Battalions of Matamoros and Jimenes.

The fourth column will be commanded by Col. Juan Morales, and in his absence, by Col. José Minon; it will be composed of the light companies of the Battalions of Matamoros and Jimenes, and the Active Battalion of San Luis."[2]

The Mexican commander even specified the number of ladders, tools, cartridge packs and spare flints to be utilized in the attack. Santa Anna's battle plan reflects his attention to detail, organization and clarity. However, his decision to attack the Alamo without support of additional artillery probably cost him more Mexican lives. But the attack, somewhat Machiavellian in its execution, was direct, quick and thorough.

Grade: A-minus

Offensive

Offensive action is necessary to achieve decisive results and to maintain freedom of action. It permits the commander to exercise initiative and impose his will upon the enemy; to set the pace and determine the course of battle; to exploit enemy weaknesses and rapidly changing situations, and to meet unexpected developments. The defensive may be forced on a commander, but it should be deliberately adopted only as a temporary expedient while awaiting an opportunity for offensive action or for the purpose of economizing forces on a front where a decision is not sought. Even on the defensive the commander seeks opportunity to seize the initiative and achieve decisive combat superiority.

Santa Anna's utilization of this principle is somewhat difficult to assess, especially since his infantry's breakthrough at the North Wall came more as a result of a combat adjustment by his field commanders (the convergence of the three major Mexican columns) than a predetermined plan. Nevertheless, Santa Anna did direct most of his troops at the Alamo's northern defenses rather than the seemingly under-defended southern positions, particularly the palisade area between the church and the South Wall. And, clearly, the North Wall breakthrough was exploited in a fastidious manner thanks to the rugged determination of the Mexican soldado. Essentially, the defense of the Alamo rested upon the maintenance of its outer wall fortifications. When the the North Wall and, subsequently, the West Wall became porous, the Alamo was doomed.

Grade: B

Mass

Superior combat power must be concentrated at the critical time and place for a decisive purpose. Superiority results from the proper combination of the elements of combat power. Proper application of the principles of mass, in conjunction with the other principles of war, may permit numerically inferior forces to achieve decisive combat superiority.

To be sure, Santa Anna did not have an "inferior" force that attacked the Alamo, although his artillery played no role in the predawn assault. His superior numbers were concentrated in such a fashion as to promote qualitative mass. (As a matter of fact, the Offensive and Mass principles are closely related in this analysis.) Texian firepower played an indirect role in the success of the Mexican Army with regard to this Principle of War. Alamo artillery fire at the northwest area of the mission–fortress forced the men under the command of Gen. Martin Perfecto de Cos to shift more to the north where they combined with the infantry columns commanded by Romero and Duque (actually Castrillon, since Duque had been wounded during the initial attack on the eastern defense of the Alamo). Clearly, Texian defenses focused on this area as some defenders from adjacent positions abandoned their initial posts to come to the aid of the comrades at the North Wall. The immediate result of such a reinforcement effort by some of the defenders left a few key areas undermanned, especially the northern portion of the West Wall. A subsequent shift to the right as a result of both Texian and "friendly fire" shifted Cos' detachment directly to that undermanned portion of the West Wall. Three Mexican columns massed at the West Wall and quickly gained entrance there. Again, the timely concentration of mass did result more from combat flexibility rather than premeditated strategy.

Grade: B

Economy of Force

Skillful and prudent use of combat power will enable the commander to accomplish the mission with minimum expenditure of resources. This principle is the corollary to the Principle of Mass. It does not imply husbanding but rather the measured allocation of available combat power to the primary task as well as secondary tasks such as limited attacks, the defense, deception or even retrograde action in order to insure sufficient combat power at the point of decision.

Santa Anna's casualties were high. Some 600 of his men were either killed or wounded—approximately one-third of his assault force. Clearly, he did not accomplish his mission "with a minimum expenditure of resources." As a matter of fact, he committed the reserves, which he commanded personally, to the leadership of Agustin Amat as soon as Texian firepower manifested itself with deadly effectiveness. Nevertheless, the armed forces under his leadership moved decisively toward their goal and achieved it in about an hour or so of combat. To be sure, Santa Anna's ultimate evaluation came at San Jacinto (and some may suggest that it came during the Mexican War a decade later), but at the Alamo—Mexico's commander-in-chief was successful.

Grade: C

Maneuver

Maneuver is an essential ingredient of combat power. It contributes materially in exploiting successes and in preserving freedom of action and reducing vulnerability. The object of maneuver is to dispose a force in such a manner as to place the enemy at a relative disadvantage and thus achieve results which would otherwise be more costly in men and material. Successful maneuver requires flexibility in organization, administrative support and command and control. It is the antithesis of permanence of location and implies avoidance of stereotyped patterns of operation.

Santa Anna's direct multicolumn assault (with superior numbers) against an inferior force in fixed defensive position does not require a complex evaluation. Still, to the credit of the men under him, Santa Anna's officers exploited battlefield changes that resulted from combat transitions, notably Texian firepower at strategic locations along the Alamo's outer defenses. Artillery fire in particular forced the column commanders, particularly those concentrated at the North Wall, to alter their initial paths of attack. And despite the chaos of the smoked-filled, predawn darkness, the Mexican soldados moved satisfactorily from position to position and achieved control of the Alamo's walls.

Grade: B

Unity of Command

The decisive application of full combat power requires unity of command. Unity of command obtains unity of effort by the coordinated action of all forces towards a common goal. While coordination may be attained by cooperation, it is best achieved by vesting a single commander with the requisite authority.

Again, Santa Anna's March 5 combat operation directive identified and explained command responsibilities, although the document did not suggest tactical responsibilities. Surprisingly, Santa Anna detailed such items as the number of flints each soldier would carry during the assault. One might assume that the Mexican commander-in-chief was either overly concerned with detail or reluctant to give his officer staff in Bexar authority to plan any aspect of the final attack. Clearly, everyone who participated in the predawn assault was aware of his role and responsibilities. Of course, he managed to exploit a relatively inferior fixed position—the Alamo's artillery park notwithstanding—with a superior mobile force. Santa Anna's efforts, and those of his field officers, with regard to this Principle of War are noteworthy. Ironically, he would violate this principle the following month at San Jacinto.

Grade: B-plus

Security

Security is essential to the preservation of combat power. Security is achieved by measures taken to preserve surprise, preserve freedom of action and deny the enemy information of friendly forces. Since risk is inherent in war, application of the principles of security does not imply undue caution and the avoidance of calculated risk. Security frequently is enhanced by bold seizure and retention of the initiative, which denies the enemy the opportunity to interfere.

Santa Anna earns his lowest grade with regard to this Principle of War. Although Mexican forces outnumbered the Alamo defenders by at least five-to-one on February 23, the first day of the siege, Santa Anna never established a proper security perimeter around the Alamo during the siege phase of his operation in Bexar. For example, during the first twenty-four hours of the siege, Albert Martin departed from the Alamo. Within two days of the beginning of the siege, Juan Seguin and Antonio Cruz y Arocha (and probably John Baylor) left the mission–fortress as couriers. Robert Brown probably left shortly after February 25 and William Oury departed on the 29th. The Gonzales Ranging Company, the so-called Gonzales 32, under the command of George C. Kimball, arrived on March 1; William Smith left the Alamo on March 3, and James B. Bonham arrived on March 3; James Allen left on March 5.

Only on the day of the final attack did Santa Anna establish a satisfactory security perimeter around the Alamo. He ordered General Joaquin Ramirez y Sesma, who had commanded the Army of the North's First Division Vanguard Brigade, to take charge of the cavalry for any potential breakout by Alamo defenders. Noted Santa Anna: "The cavalry, under Colonel Joaquin Ramirez y Sesma, will be stationed at the Alameda, saddling up at 3 o'clock A. M. It shall be its duty to scout the country, to prevent the possibility of escape." As he had planned for, an attempted organized escape took place. Second lieutenant Manuel Loranca in the Dolores Cavalry regiment noted that "sixty-two Texians who sallied from the east side of the fort were received by the lancers and all killed. Only one of these made resistance; a very active man, armed with a double barrel gun and a single barrel pistol, with which he killed a corporal of the lancers named Eugenio. These were all killed by the lance, except one, who ensconced himself under a bush and it was necessary to shoot him."[3]

Grade: D

Surprise

Surprise can decisively shift the balance of combat power. By surprise, success out of proportion to the effort expended may be obtained. Surprise results from striking an enemy at a time, place, and in a manner for which he is not prepared. It is not essential for the enemy to be taken unaware but only that he becomes aware too late to react effectively. Factors contributing to surprise include speed, deception, application of unexpected combat power, effective intelligence and counterintelligence, to include communication ... and variations in tactics and methods of operation.

The termination of Mexican artillery on March 5 was a signal of sorts to the Alamo garrison that after twelve days of periodic cannon blasts, Santa Anna was probably shifting his strategy from that of a siege operation to an assault. Instead of altering his defensive strategy to one of heightened anticipation, Travis seemingly tolerated subsequent periods of reduced alertness. Therefore, Travis' inactions indirectly underscored Santa Anna's utilization of the Principle of War.

Santa Anna's forces placed themselves quite close to the Alamo during the earliest hours of March 6, which furthered the mobility of the Mexican infantry since they would have less distance to travel to reach the exterior walls. As a result, the element of surprise was utilized rather effectively by Santa Anna. And despite the initiation of the attack by enthusiastic soldados who shouted "Viva Santa Anna" and therefore curbed the parallel concept of "total surprise," the Alamo was nonetheless taken by "surprise." For example, the South gate lunette probably fell with little resistance.

Grade: B

Simplicity

Simplicity contributes to successful operations. Direct, simple plans and clear, concise orders minimize misunderstanding and confusion, if other factors are equal, the simplest plan is preferred.

Once again, Santa Anna's battle plan orders of March 5 are noteworthy. They are indeed simple, precise (in fact, too precise with regard to certain points) and direct. Perhaps the simplest plan would have been one that emphasized a longer siege and utilized more artillery fire. However, a longer siege could have been less effective considering Santa Anna's poor implementation of the principle of security. After all, Col. James Fannin commanded a sizable force at Goliad and the Alamo received a message from Robert Williamson at Gonzales dated March 1, which urged Travis to "hold out until we can assist you." Nevertheless these are speculative observations that have little or nothing to do with the historical process.

Grade: A-minus

Overall Evaluation: B

Notes

1. Maurice Matloff, ed. *American Military History* (Washington, D.C.: Office of the Center of Military History, United States Army, 1969), 6-7. The field manuals used by Matloff have since been revised. As a result, the wording of several principles has changed slightly.
2. Santa Anna order in John H. Jenkins, ed. *The Papers of the Texas Revolution, 1835-1836*, Austin, TX (1973), IV, 518-519.
3. *San Antonio Express*, June 23, 1878.

ABOUT THE ARTIST

Howard Bender

Howard Bender is a New Jersey-based, professional freelance illustrator who has created artwork for numerous clients during the last twenty-five years. He illustrated his first *Alamo Journal* cover in July 1995 for issue no. 97. That cover illustration later appeared in *The Davy Crockett Almanac & Book of Lists*.

He has provided artwork for textbooks, newspapers, storybooks, advertising displays, storyboards, coloring books, libraries, comics and such publications as *Time* magazine and *Children's Better Health*, among others.

Bender is best known for his illustrations that have been distributed by such familiar comic book publishers as Disney, Marvel, DC, Archie, Harvey, and Topps.

He has created a number of works that have included a list of familiar licensed comic book characters ranging from Superman and Spiderman to Richie Rich and the Flintstones. Bender has also created such original cartoon characterizations as "Mr. Fixitt," the "Sherlock Holmes Minute Mysteries," and "Billy & Pop!"

Bender, who has also been trained in computer art and design, has lectured and taught at various educational institutions and libraries over the years.

Through his firm, Dynamic Illustrations & Caricatures, Bender created and developed the popular Internet website "Davy Crockett Craze," a nostalgic salute to Walt Disney's *Davy Crockett, King of the Wild Frontier*, which starred Fess Parker.

$5.00

THE ALAMO JOURNAL

ISSUE #117
JUNE 2000

The Official Publication of THE ALAMO SOCIETY

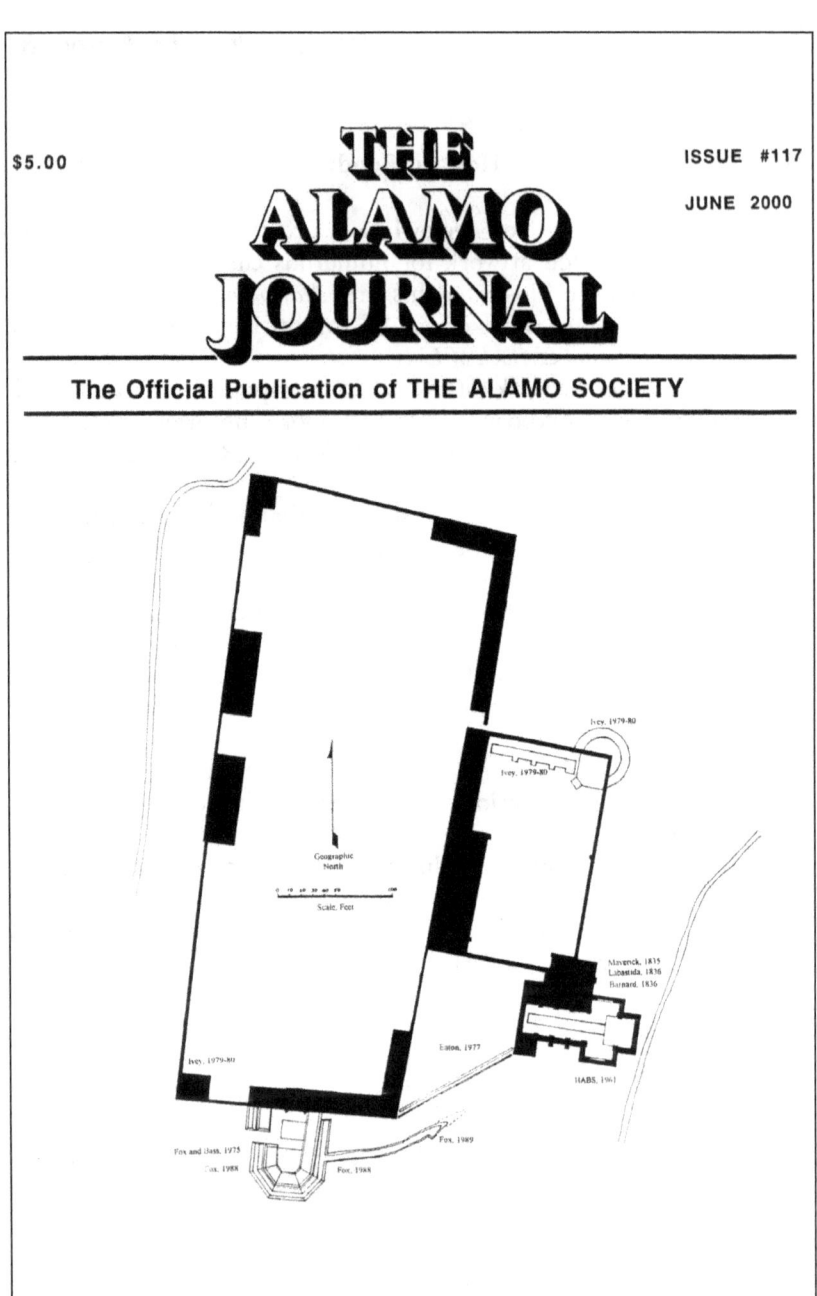

"Alamo Map" by James E. Ivey, Alamo Journal, no. 117 (June 2000).

Archeological Evidence for the Defenses of the Alamo

by James E. Ivey

Although the Battle of the Alamo is what everyone hears about, you don't see any traces of the defenses of the place in Alamo Plaza today. In downtown San Antonio, in the middle of heavy traffic, it's difficult to imagine that this was once an isolated mission standing on an empty grassy plain across the river from the town, where several thousand people fought a bloody battle in 1836. But beneath the streets, sidewalks and grass of Alamo Plaza, traces of the defenses of the Alamo survived the urbanization of the area.

The South Gate

In 1975, plans for the improvement of the small urban park area in front of the Alamo gave Anne Fox of the Center for Archaeological Research at the University of Texas at San Antonio a chance to look for the remains of the Low Barracks, the gateway building along the south wall of the Alamo. Within a few days, the excavators found sections of massive limestone wall foundations, and a trench with a scattering of lead musket and rifle balls, cannon shell fragments, and other military debris lying in the bottom. It was clear that they had relocated the foundations of the Low Barracks and the south gate defensive trench.[1]

At this point, archaeologists realized that the survival of portions of the defenses in the earth could tell us the truth about the plan of the defenses of the Alamo. No good, unquestioned map of the defenses was known to exist. All the available maps were made at various times after the battle, and all disagreed with each other in so many ways that none could be trusted. The archaeologists thought that the evidence in the ground, if enough survived, might allow us to arrive at some idea of the actual defensive plan of the Alamo, and therefore indicate which map actually recorded that defensive plan. Having a plan we could trust would be a big step in the direction of resolving some of the mysteries of the Battle of the Alamo.

After three seasons of excavation, the second and third in 1988 and 1989 during a second landscaping project, the plan of the south gate defenses became fairly clear.[2] Landscaping before 1975 had destroyed much of the physical evidence, so that the actual ground surface at the time of the battle was gone, scraped away by earthmoving in the century and a half since the battle. As a result, no traces of the defensive parapets built using the earth from the trenches remained (although some posthole patterns suggested that traces of stockade revetments might be found with the right sort of excavation)—but the lower portions of the trenches survived.

The surviving sections of the trenches were straight, flat-bottomed, and smooth-walled, militarily correct and generally following the standard textbook rules for such trenches.[3] If we assume that was the case with the earthworks built aboveground, as well, then by applying those same rules, we may arrive at a probable reconstruction of the defensive structures.

The South Wall Trench

In 1988, the archaeologists noticed a gap in the east wall of the south gate trench, and in 1989 the fieldwork followed this trench eastward, across the width of the south wall. The trench continued around the probable location of the southeastern corner, as it was shown on most maps.[4] Immediately east of the corner, however, it widened abruptly by about a meter. The trench continued with the wider cross section for only two or three meters, and then tapered into a narrow, shallow, round-bottomed trench.[5] Clearly, the last excavation units were very near the end of the trench. This evidence indicates that the trench only extended perhaps five or six meters northeast of the southeastern corner, rather than all the way to the church, as it was traditionally thought.

The Southeastern Stockade

Jack Eaton, of the Center for Archeological Research at the University of Texas at San Antonio, conducted excavations as part of repaving the area in front of the church in 1977. Among other things, his excavations found the remains of two trenches that had been associated with the stockade wall, running from the southwest corner of the church to the southeast corner of the south gate building.[6] Here, the maps agreed that there had been some sort of stockaded defensive structure, but disagreed on its plan.

The two trenches Eaton found were 6 feet apart. The northern ditch was about 2.5 feet wide and 18 inches or so of its depth survived.[7] The second trench, 6 feet south of the first, was much narrower, and consisted of a U-shaped ditch about 9 inches across and 18 inches deep, with a series of post molds at about 2-foot intervals along its south face. It was clear that we had found something like the stockade defense illustrated by J. B. Wheeler in his 1882 manual, *Elements of Fortification*.[8]

This cross-section view shows a structure that would have left an archaeological record very like what we found, with the rear trench serving as a step-down and the source of earth to make the banquette against the stockade face. The posts at intervals along the face of the stockade covered gaps left in the main row of logs, and stood perhaps two feet shorter than these logs. This would form loopholes for rifle or musket fire. A larger ditch was to have been excavated along the outside of the stockade, and the earth from it packed against the exterior of the logs to protect them from musket and cannon fire to some extent.

If the standard practice for this sort of fortification was followed, then the stockade stood to a height of about 8 feet. The loopholes were probably about 2 feet high, with the bottom of each gap about 6 feet above the ground. The banquette would have been about 1.75 feet high, giving a height of 4.25 feet from the top of the banquette to the bottom of the loopholes. The banquette was perhaps 2 feet wide. The logs of the stockade were supposed to extend about 3 feet into the ground, but the actual depth of the stockade trench in units 4, 7, and 12 below the probable surface of the courtyard at the time of the battle was a little less than 2 feet.

In San Antonio, Cos built parapets like the one being described here across the entrance of each street into the main plazas of the town. J. E. Field, who helped take them, described these parapets in 1836: "a ditch was dug ten feet wide, five feet deep, raised on the inner side [to form a parapet], so as to make an elevation of ten feet. Over this was erected a breastwork of perpendicular posts, with portholes for muskets, and one in the center for cannon."[9] Such a stockade was generally used to protect the defenders against small-arms fire; it was not intended to offer much resistance to artillery.[10] However, if the exterior earth parapet was made thick enough, 8 or 9 feet, then the stockade wall becomes a timber revetment for a parapet, and could resist artillery like any other earthen parapet. The difference between the two depends on the size of the ditch excavated in front to supply the earthen protective blanket, as discussed in the previous section. Because this ditch was apparently never completed, the stockade remained just that, probably without any exterior earth blanket at all for most of its length, making it vulnerable to cannon fire.

The traditional picture of the stockade, as presented by Eaton, described it as consisting of "two rows of cedar posts spaced six feet apart and set within shallow trenches. The posts in each row were tied together top and bottom with rawhide strips, with the earth rammed around the base. A long, deep ditch was then dug in front [of] the double palisade, and the excavated earth was packed between the rows of piles."[11] Eaton's description, however, has no support in the documents. Eaton cited Frederick C. Chabot, *The Alamo: Mission, Fortress and Shrine* as the authority for this description of the stockade.[12] Chabot, however, did not describe the Alamo stockade in Eaton's terms; instead, he said "[t]he entrenchment to protect the front of the chapel which faced west, and the south side of the garrison, or old monastery, consisted of a ditch and breastworks, and a cedar-post stockade."[13] Chabot's description of the Alamo defenses does not mention two rows of posts six feet apart with earth between them, or any other of the details Eaton gave. Rather, Eaton's detailed description of a stockade was taken from earlier in Chabot, where he described the construction of a stockade around the front of the parish church in the town plaza of San Antonio, not at the Alamo.[14] During the siege of Bexar, Cos had made the church of Nuestra Señora de Candelaria, on Town Plaza, into his magazine and powder house. On October 22, James Bowie and J. W. Fannin reported to General Austin that behind the stockade parapets at the mouths of the streets into the main plazas, described by J. E. Field, above, the Mexican army had "8 pieces (4 lb) mounted—and one of larger size preparing for us. They have none on the Church—but have removed all their ammunition to it, and enclosed it by a wall, made of wood, six feet apart and six feet high, filled in with dirt, extending from the corners to the ditch, say sixty yards in length ..."[15] This structure, however, was not a defensive position, but rather a "bomb-proof" or "splinter-proof" protective wall, designed to shelter explosives from being impacted by incoming shells, ball, or shrapnel.[16]

Eaton used the Theodore Gentilz painting of the battle of the Alamo, Eaton's Figure 2, to show the structure he thought was at the southwest corner of the church. Where Gentilz got this idea of the construction of the stockade is unknown.[17] No nineteenth-century description of any historical value agrees with him or with Eaton.

In 1992, Herbert Uecker reviewed the literature for descriptions of the stockade fortifications of the Alamo.[18] Uecker stated that Eaton's excavations "revealed rather conclusively that the palisade was comprised of a double row of timbers," and that his work "invalidat[ed] Ivey's ... single-row theory."[19] However, Eaton's fieldwork, rather than invalidating the idea of a single row of stockade, provided the evidence that prompted me to suggest it in the first place.

Uecker cited Reuben Potter as describing the stockade as Eaton presented it, but in reality Potter said: "The intrenchment (R) consisted of a ditch and breastwork, the latter of earth packed between two rows of palisades, the outer row being higher than the earthwork."[20] At first, this sounds like what Eaton was describing, but after some thought we realize that the phrase "the outer row being higher than the earthwork" makes this, instead, a description of a standard stockaded defense with an earthen firing step revetted by vertical logs, more or less as illustrated by Wheeler, and again does not present the picture given by Eaton. Worse, this was an enhanced version of Potter's original discussion of the Battle of the Alamo in 1860, in which he had less to say about the stockade: "(R) an entrenchment running from the south-west angle of the chapel to the gate. This work was not manned against the assault."[21]

In addition to the lack of documentary support for such a structure, there are physical problems with it, as well. The obvious one is that the stockaded structure Eaton described, six feet thick with earth packed between two lines of posts set in the ground, could not have been built anyway, because, as we have seen, the ditch was never excavated beyond about twenty feet from the southeast corner of the Plaza. As a result, there would have been no earth to fill the space between the rows of logs. As Uecker points out, "without the soil packing, the rows of timbers would have provided little resistance to fire from Mexican artillery pieces."[22] Even had the stockade been built, however, such a defense would have created an area on its exterior which did not receive fire from the interior unless the defenders climbed on top of the parapet. This would have exposed them to fire from the enemy, as Gen. Vicente Filisola described in a similar circumstance on the north wall.[23] Mahan, in fact, specifically discouraged the use of two rows of posts six feet apart and filled with packed earth as a defense against artillery fire: "This method has been tried, and is less solid than the one here laid down," that is, two layers of timbers placed in contact, totaling two feet in thickness.[24] If the interior row of posts had been made lower so that firing embrasures could be built through the wall, the result is the structure Potter described, virtually the same as the standard stockade.

In other words, other than a graphic representation by Theodore Gentilz, in a painting with innumerable other errors, Eaton and Uecker have no documentation of any sort to support the idea of a double-row stockade filled with earth, which also violates basic military principles and common sense, while the single row stockade is shown on the maps of Ignacio Labastida and José Juan Sánchez Navarro, mentioned in Filisola's study of the Texas War and on Sánchez-Navarro's index to his map, fits the archaeological evidence, and matches standard military practice. It is clear that Eaton and Uecker's description of the stockade along this face of the Alamo defenses cannot be accepted.[25]

The Southwest Corner

I was field director of the Radio Shack excavations in 1979-1980, when we looked at a strip of land just north of the southwest corner of the Alamo, 20 feet wide and running 88 feet west from just east of the ruined buildings at the corner across the realigned acequia that ran parallel to the west wall of the fortifications.[26] Ignacio Labastida shows no exterior trenches or other defenses outside the west wall at the southwest corner, other than the acequia along the outside of the wall and a gun platform in barbette in the southwest corner itself, on a high platform that allowed the gun to fire over the top of the walls.[27] José Juan Sánchez Navarro, a Mexican officer who drew two slightly different maps in 1836 and about 1840, shows several defensive structures outside the wall in this area: the Plano has a long, straight trench along the west half of the south wall, around the southwest corner, and north for nearly half the length of the wall, where it ends against a semicircular trench structure against the center area of the wall. The Fuerte plan shows the same semicircular trench at the center of the west wall, but instead of the long straight trench along the south and west sides of the southwest corner, this plan shows a second large semicircular trench just north of the corner itself.[28]

The excavations found that none of the defenses shown by Sanchez-Navarro on the outside of the west wall just north of the corner were actually present—the relatively even, slightly sloping ground outside the wall ran from the acequia up to the wall itself with no interruptions. This agrees with Labastida's depiction of the corner. The archaeological evidence does show that the new ditch for the acequia, which had originally flowed along the interior of the west wall, was excavated about the same time as the battle of the Alamo—that is, the new ditch was dug from the same ground surface on which the battle of the Alamo was fought. The physical evidence, historical documents, and artifacts all indicate a construction date of between 1829 and 1836, making it virtually certain that the acequia was moved by Ugartechea's engineers from within the fortification to its new alignment along the west wall in 1835 as part of the defensive system of the site.[29] This move achieved two things: first, it placed a moat-like ditch along the west wall; and second, it allowed the old openings for the original acequia path through the north and south walls to be closed. It is possible that Sanchez-Navarro's series of earthworks was based on a bad sketch and poor recollection of the acequia as some sort of series of trenches along the west wall.

The North Courtyard

In 1979 and 1980, I conducted a series of excavations in the north courtyard of the Alamo as part of the reconstruction of an enclosing wall here, separating the grounds from the streets along the line of the wall that had stood here during the battle. Preservation was better in this area than at the South Gate, but once again we found that landscaping had removed the ground surface from the period of the battle. Our excavations found a large trench, surprisingly wide and deep. John Greer's excavations in the area in the 1960s had found the same thing, but had not recognized it—his interpretation of this area was very confused.[30] This trench was in the same location as a trench in the north courtyard shown by Labastida.

Soon afterward, we found a similar trench in the area of the northeastern corner of the Alamo, near the wide trench of the north courtyard.[31] This trench was either on the corner of the northeastern yard, or just outside it on the east, depending on which location of the east wall you chose from the various maps. However, there was a distinct curve to the two faces of this ditch. I knew that Labastida's map showed a circular trench just outside the northeastern corner of the Alamo, part of the defenses of a low cannon platform in this corner. I immediately suspected I had found that circular trench. With careful measurements we were able to show that the plan was circular and centered on the location of the corner of the northeastern wall as shown on Labastida's plan.

The Church

A final piece of physical evidence about the defenses of the Alamo has been preserved by the surviving walls of the church itself. These walls stood to a height of about thirty feet when the Mexican Army began the fortification of the Alamo. Col. Domingo de Ugartechea, who directed the construction of the defenses, decided to put the sixteen-pounder in the head of the church, at its east end in the space above where the altar would have been, had the building ever been finished. This gun position was to be a *bateria caballero*, or "cavalier" battery, a high battery commanding a large area to the northeast, east, and southeast of the church. This, as the Labastida map shows, was a battery in barbette, giving the sixteen-pounder the greatest width of field of fire. Samuel Maverick, a prisoner in San Antonio at the time, witnessed this construction, and later described how the army "threw down the arches [ribs] of the church ... in order to make an inclined plane to haul cannon on top of the church." In his journal entry for October 26, 1835, he said that "an 18 pounder [actually 16 pounds] just mounted. Was carried by to the Alamo, and raised to the top of the church ..."[32] With the demolition of the ribs and the small area of completed vaulting, combined with the stone rubble in the convento courtyard, there was enough material to build such a battery—except for one problem: the east wall of the church was too high for the ramp to fit within the length of the church.

The Church was 98 feet long from the inside edge of the

front door on the west to the base of the wall on the east. A battery that would permit firing in two or three directions required a width of about 25 feet, which fit easily into the sanctuary interior width of 27 feet, and a depth of 24 feet, which extended beyond the 17-foot depth of the sanctuary, 7 feet into the transept. A battery length of 24 feet left only 74 feet of the interior of the church for the ramp. A wall height of 30 feet required a battery height of 27.25 feet for guns in barbette. This would need a ramp 163.5 feet long, following the standard fortification rule for cannon ramps of 6 feet of horizontal distance for each foot of altitude gained. Since the nave was only 98 feet long, it was clearly impossible to fit such a long ramp into the building. Either the front of the church would have to be removed, or the east wall would have to be lowered. Ugartechea elected to lower the east wall, keeping the gun position enclosed within the massive church so as to have the protected interior defensive position that he wanted. A ramp length of 74 feet could reach no higher than 12.33 feet, which meant that for a barbette battery, with its standard parapet of 2.75 feet in height, the east wall had to be lowered to a height of 15.08 feet. In fact, the surviving structure of the church shows that the east wall was torn down to this height. The lowest portion, on the north side, is about 14.5 feet high, and the highest, on the south, is about 15.75 feet high. Most of the east side is fairly level at about 15 feet high.[33] Descriptions at the time indicate that the ramp ran from the battery all the way down to the main west door of the church.[34] The lowering of the east wall to the precise height required by a battery platform of standard size and a ramp of standard slope is direct proof that the Mexican engineers were following the rules of field fortification current in 1836.

The available rubble from the demolished ribs, vault, and part of the massive east wall, along with debris from the collapsed walls of the convento courtyard, was enough for the construction of the ramp or the battery platform, but not both. One of the two was built of timbers. If we take Maverick's description literally, then the ramp for the platform was built with the rubble, indicating that the gun platform was built entirely of timber—but this seems unlikely, since the platform receives a great deal of stress when the gun is fired. Another eyewitness, Dr. J. H.

Barnard, specifically described the timber ramp in the church as it burned after the Battle of San Jacinto: "a platform had been built extending from the great door to the top of the wall on the back side for the purpose of taking up the artillery to the top of the church. This was made of wood..."[35] This tells us that Maverick was being imprecise when he implied that the rubble from the church was used to build the "inclined plane" of the ramp.

The Plan of the Defenses of the Alamo as shown by Archaeology

Combining the results of all the archaeology and our examination of the church gives us a plan of the defenses of the Alamo as shown by archaeology.[36] This plan doesn't look at all like the maps made by Reuben Marmaduke Potter in the 1840s, supposedly one of the best sketches of the defenses of the Alamo.[37] Nor does it look like the drawings of Sánchez-Navarro. We don't know if it looks like the Green Jameson map, because the only version of that map we have was created by Adina de Zavala and Jane Briscoe about 1911, using Briscoe's memory and a tracing of one of Giraud's plans as its basis.[38]

What it looks like is the Ignacio Labastida plan. In fact, only the Labastida plan shows all the trenches on our archaeological plan of the Alamo, and does not show ditches where we found none. As a result of the archaeology, then, we can say that the Alamo defenses followed the standard military field fortification practices of the 1830s, and that they were fairly accurately recorded by the Labastida plan, but not on any other known map.

Finally, we can say that one specific plan is a good representation of the defenses of the Alamo, which gives us a standard against which to measure other maps. This, in conjunction with a detailed search into land ownership records and previously underused letters and journals of Mexican officers and enlisted men who fought at the Alamo, is allowing a surprisingly detailed new reconstruction of the structures standing at the time of the Battle of the Alamo, and the course of the battle itself.

Notes

1. Anne A. Fox, Feris A. Bass, Jr., and Thomas R. Hester, *Archaeology and History of Alamo Plaza*, Center for Archaeological Research, Archaeological Survey Report No. 16 (San Antonio: University of Texas at San Antonio, 1976), 36, fig. 12.

2. Anne A. Fox, *Archaeological Investigations in Alamo Plaza, San Antonio, Bexar County, Texas, 1988 and 1989*, Center for Archaeological Research, Archaeological Survey Report No. 205 (San Antonio: University of Texas at San Antonio, 1992), 21, fig. 6.

3. D. H. Mahan, *A Complete Treatise on Field Fortification* (New York: Wiley and Long, 1836), and J. B. Wheeler, *The Elements of Fortification for the Use of the Cadets of the United States Military Academy at West Point, N. Y.* (New York: D. Van Nostrand, 1882). Coincidentally, the illustrations for the 1836 Mahan volume were drawn by Lieutenant J. E. Blake (p. x), who later, in the 1840s, was stationed at the Alamo, where he drew a perspective view of the structures in 1845, and one of the better plans of the mission buildings and plaza in 1849; see George Nelson, *The Alamo: An Illustrated History*, (first ed.; Dry Frio Canyon, Texas: Aldine Press, 1998), 60, 68.

4. Fox, *Investigations*, 27, fig. 10.

5. Anne A. Fox, 1989 Field School, profile drawings, units E1004N1991, E1004N1992, E1004N1993, on file at the Center for Archaeological Research, University of Texas at San Antonio, San Antonio, Texas.

6. Jack Eaton, *Excavations at the Alamo Shrine (Mission San Antonio de Valero)*, Center for Archaeological Research, Special Report No. 10 (San Antonio: University of Texas at San Antonio, 1980), 24-25, 47, figs. 3, 10, 11.

7. Eaton, *Alamo Shrine*, 24-25, 47, figs. 3, 10, 11.

8. Wheeler, *Elements of Fortification*, 161; see also Mahan, *Treatise*, 93.

9. J. E. Field, *Three Years in Texas* (Greenfield, Massachusetts: Justin Jones, 1836), 17.

10. Wheeler, *Elements*, 161.

11. Eaton, *Alamo Shrine*, 8, 25, 47.

12. Frederick C. Chabot, *The Alamo: Mission, Fortress and Shrine* (San Antonio: Frederick C. Chabot, 1941), 24. This is the same description as presented by Chabot in earlier versions of this booklet, in 1936, 1935, and 1931.

13. Chabot, *The Alamo*, 28 (not 24, as Eaton cited it). Chabot gives no references, and the source of this description is unknown.

14. Chabot, *The Alamo*, 26.

15. James Bowie and J. W. Fannin to General S. F. Austin, Mission Espada, October 22, 1835, in John H. Jenkins, ed. *The Papers of the Texas Revolution 1835-1836*, volume 2 (Austin: Jay A. Matthews, 1973), 190-91; compare with Chabot, *The Alamo*, 26.

16. Mahan, *Treatise*, 189-91; Wheeler, *Elements*, 135-143.

17. Nelson, *Illustrated History*, 79. The Gentilz painting was made about 1885, and contains innumerable major structural errors.

18. Uecker, "Archival Investigations Regarding the Alamo Lunette and Palisade," in Fox, *Investigations*, 16.

19. Uecker, "Alamo Lunette and Palisade," 16.
20. Reuben M. Potter, *The Fall of the Alamo*, Old South Leaflets no. 130, 1933, 92 (not p. 91, as cited by Uecker), John Peace Library Special Collections, University of Texas at San Antonio. This article was originally printed in *Magazine of American History, 1878*, with the description of the stockade on p. 3.
21. Reuben M. Potter, *The Fall of the Alamo: a Reminiscence of the Revolution of Texas* (San Antonio: Herald Steam Press, 1860), 8.
22. Uecker, "Alamo Lunette and Palisade," 16.
23. Vicente Filisola, *Memoirs for the History of the War In Texas*, Wallace Woolsey, tr. (Austin: Eakin Press, 1987), vol. 2, 171; Vicente Filisola, *Memorias para la Historia de la Guerra de Tejas* (2 vols.; Mexico City: Tipografía de R. Rafael, 1849), vol. 2, 385.
24. Mahan, *Treatise*, 97, 100.
25. Ygnacio de Labastida, "Plano de la Ciudad de S[a]n Antonio de Bejar y fortificacion del Alamo," Map Collection, Center for American History, University of Texas at Austin; a good black and white reproduction is in Nelson, *Illustrated History*, 23-24. Ignacio Labastida was a colonel under General Vicente Filisola, and was commander of the engineers. José Juan Sanchez-Navarro, "Ayudantía de Inspección de Nuevo León y Tamaulípas," 2 vols., with one plan of the Alamo, the "Fuerte de S[a]n Antonio de Valero;" José Juan Sánchez, the "Plano Del Fuerte, Su Esplicacion I Algunas Notas," on the photostat of the "Copia del Mapa ... sacada del original por José Juan Sánchez Estrada, Coronel de Ejercite ... 1840," cataloged as the "Mapa de los Estados de Parras," Map M972.13 1828a2, in the Benson Latin American Collection (BLAC); for a good copy and a complete transcript and translation of the captions and indexes, see Jack Jackson and James Ivey, "Mystery Artist of the Alamo: José Juan Sánchez," *Southwest Historical Quarterly* 105 (October 2001) 2:207-253; also in Nelson, *Illustrated History*, 21 (the Fuerte plan), 22 (the Plano and Vista). Helen Hunnicutt published a good copy of the Fuerte plan in "A Mexican View of the Texas War," *The Library Chronicle of the University of Texas*, 4 (summer 1951) 2:59-74. Nelson's publication of the Plano was the first since Carlos Sanchez-Navarro y Peón published it for the first time in *La Guerra de Tejas, Memorias de un Soldado* (Mexico City: Editorial Polis, 1938), following page 96.
26. James Ivey, "Radio Shack Ground Plan, Excavated Features," Radio Shack Excavations Field Notes, 1979-1980, on file at the Center for Archaeological Research, University of Texas at San Antonio, San Antonio, Texas.
27. Labastida, "Plano ... del Alamo," J.
28. Sanchez-Navarro, "Fuerte," J; Sánchez, "Plano," 23.
29. The ditch was dug after the Treviño grant of 1829, which states that the old ditch down the Plaza was still in use then; see Spanish Government to Alexandro Treviño, December 31, 1828-April 20, 1829, Bexar County Deed Records, vol. F2, 206-208. The exterior ditch was in existence at the time of the battle, as shown on the Labastida map. The new ditch went out of use soon after 1850, became largely filled with dirt and trash, and was then re-excavated

and returned to use in the late 1800s, along a slightly different course. At the Radio Shack excavations, the two ditches overlapped somewhat, but were two clearly distinct structures.

30. James E. Ivey and Anne A. Fox, *Archaeological and Historical Investigations at the Alamo North Wall, San Antonio, Bexar County, Texas*, Center for Archaeological Research, Archaeological Survey Report no. 224 (San Antonio: The University of Texas at San Antonio, 1997) unit D, 17-20, 35-36, fig. 9. John W. Greer, *A Description of the Stratigraphy, Features, and Artifacts from an Archaeological Excavation at the Alamo*, Archaeological Program Report no. 3 (Austin: Texas State Building Commission,1967), feature 1, areas A and B, 5, 6, 38.

31. Ivey and Fox, *North Wall*, units E, EII, 20-23, fig. 10.

32. Thomas Ricks Lindley has demonstrated that the cannon being placed by Mexican forces in late 1835 was an iron sixteen-pounder, not the eighteen-pounder, which was brought in later by Texan forces; Thomas Ricks Lindley, "Alamo Artillery: Number, Type, Caliber and Concussion," *Alamo Journal*, 82 (July 1992):7n6. Samuel Maverick mistakenly thought the Mexican cannon was an eighteen-pounder. Samuel Maverick, *Samuel Maverick, Texan, 1803-1870: A Collection of Letters, Journals and Memoirs*, Rena Maverick Green, ed. (San Antonio: Rena Maverick Green, 1952), 32; Samuel Maverick to Captain S. M. Howe, July 3, 1847, in Green, *Samuel Maverick, Texan*, 323-25, and in Rena Maverick Green, *Memoirs of Mary A. Maverick* (San Antonio: Alamo Printing Co., 1921), 133-34. In "Mapping the Alamo," Rod Timanus quotes the next sentence from Maverick's 1847 letter, which indicates that by that year Maverick could not recall whether fortifications were built before or after the fall of the Alamo in 1836—but his diary entries made at the time leave no doubt that the construction occurred in October 1835; Rod Timanus, "Mapping the Alamo," *Alamo Journal* 108 (March, 1998):5.

33. W. Eugene George, James Emmerich, and José Jiménez, "Mission San Antonio de Valero (the Alamo), San Antonio, Bexar County, Texas," TEX 318, Historic American Buildings Survey, August, 1961, sheet 7.

34. Labastida, "Plano . . . del Alamo," Y; Sanchez-Navarro,"Fuerte," c; Sánchez, "Plano," 19; Filisola, *Memoirs*, vol. 2, 83; Filisola, *Memorias*, vol. 2, 182-85; Joseph H. Barnard, *The Journal of J. H. Barnard: A Composite of Known Versions . . .* , Hobart Huson, ed. (Refugio, Texas: n.p., 1949), 44-45.

35. Barnard, *Journal*, 44-45.

36. The base plan of the Alamo used for this map is my reconstruction, based on the François Giraud survey of the Plaza in 1849-1850. Giraud's survey of the entire Plaza is no longer available, but he left enough notes on his other plans to allow that survey to be reconstructed.

37. Potter, *The Fall of the Alamo*, 92 (not p. 91, as cited by Uecker).

38. Schoelwer, "The Artist's Alamo," 411. Briscoe had seen the original Jameson map many years previously, before it was apparently destroyed. Rather than Briscoe "tracing" the plan from the original, as Schoelwer says, she and Zavala roughed out a sketch plan of the Alamo on which they attempted to relocate the various letter designations given by Jameson as Briscoe remembered them. This very poor sketch plan is on two pieces of

paper in the de Zavala (Adina) collection, Box 2M209, Center for American History, University of Texas at Austin. Zavala transferred this guesswork plan to a copy of Giraud's map of the Alamo and used that as the Jameson map in her book, *History and Legends of the Alamo and Other Missions in and around San Antonio* (San Antonio: n.p., 1917), 29.

ABOUT THE ARTICLE'S AUTHOR

James E. Ivey

James E. Ivey is the Research Historian for the History Program of the Intermountain Cultural Resource Center of the Intermountain Regional Office, National Park Service in Sante Fe, New Mexico.

He was a contract historical archaeologist in Texas for ten years and has specialized in the cultural and architectural history of the American Southwest. As an archaeologist and historian, Ivey has worked on Spanish missions, presidios, ranches, and the history of ranching and settlements from Texas to California, as well as American frontier forts, industrial sites and settlements.

As an architectural historian, Ivey has written the structural histories and coauthored the cultural landscape studies of the four San Antonio missions and the Alamo in Texas. In addition, he has written the structural histories of the colonial periods of the four missions of Salinas Pueblo Missions National Monument, the missions and other Spanish structures at Pecos National Historical Park, and the missions at Jemez Springs State Park in New Mexico. Ivey has also carried out architectural surveys of two presidios and a mission in northern Mexico, and is writing the architectural histories of the three missions of Tumacacori National Monument in Arizona.

He presented a paper titled "The Defenses of the Alamo as Found by Archeology" at the 2000 Alamo Society Symposium in San Antonio. The paper was printed in issue no. 117 of *The Alamo Journal* in June 2000.

Ivey is presently working on architectural histories of nineteenth century ranching buildings at Salinas Pueblo Missions National Monument and comparative architectural studies of the entire northern Franciscan frontier from 1565 to 1821.

"Davy Crockett" by Howard Bender, Alamo Journal, no. 107 (December 1997).

Where Did Davy Die?

by Robert L. Durham

• "With his rifle, 'Betsy,' Davy Crockett and the twelve from Tennessee held the inner gate to the little courtyard, firing until they no longer had time to load. Then clubbing their rifles and drawing hunting knives from their belts, they dispatched twenty-five more of the enemy before the last backwoodsman fell."[1]

• "David Crockett and his Tennesseans, charged with the defense of the court, were trapped in the open fight for their death fight. Some may have tried to reach the chapel, and one or two may have succeeded before its doors were of necessity barred. Crockett himself, however, attempted to gain the southern barracks but got no farther than the eastern end of it. Unable to attain a haven, he and a few others had huddled together to kill while they could."[2]

• "Crockett died outdoors, where he wished to be be. When the firing was over, he and his men were found at their assigned post near the stockade fence."[3]

• "Crockett's Tennesseans, at bar near the palisade, battled with a wild fury that awed even the attackers."[4]

Stirring stuff, but is it accurate? New revisionist wisdom holds that Crockett surrendered and was executed by order of Santa Anna, although there is no concrete evidence to prove this. Traditionalists hold that the famous frontiersman died defending the courtyard in front of the church. Both the traditionalists and the revisionists usually agree that his post was in this area, behind the stockade palisade running from the eastern edge of the South Wall to the southwest corner of the church. This has been stated so often and in so many secondary sources that it is often taken as established fact.

Even artists have gotten into the act. There are many depictions of the "last stand" of Crockett and his Tennesseans with the Alamo church in the background. This makes for a much more dramatic and easily recognizable image than showing a nondescript adobe wall in the background. As in Lewis Carroll's *The Hunting of the Snark*, the more often something is stated and depicted the more authoritative it becomes:

> Just the place for a Snark! I have said
>   it twice:
> That alone should encourage the crew.
> Just the place for a Snark! I have said
>   it thrice:
> What I tell you three times is true.

The only primary evidence that assigns David Crockett to the defense of the stockade is the account by Dr. John Sutherland: "Colonel Crockett ... remarked to him [Travis], 'Colonel, here I am. Assign me a position, and I and my twelve boys will try and defend it.' Travis replied that he wanted him to defend the picket wall extending from the end of the barracks, on the south side, to the corner of the church."[5]

The Sutherland account presents several problems. First, Crockett did not have "twelve boys." The Tennessee Mounted Volunteers, in which Crockett was enlisted as a private, was commanded by Capt. William B. Harrison, with Lt. Robert Campbell as the second in command.[6] According to Sutherland, Travis offered Crockett a command upon his arrival at Bexar but the former congressman replied that "all the honor that I desire is that of defending as a high private, in common with my fellow-citizens, the liberties of our common country."[7]

A second problem with the Sutherland account rests with the nature of Travis himself. The chance of Travis undermining Harrison and Campbell by assigning Crockett to the command of their company, is negligible. As a regular army officer, Travis would probably never have made such an offer. Furthermore, in an unpublished essay, Thomas Ricks Lindley has put forth some rather convincing arguments that cast major doubts on the veracity of Dr. Sutherland's personal account.[8]

Travis, in a letter of Sam Houston, said: "The Hon. David Crockett was seen at all points, animating the men to do their duty."[9] This may suggest that Crockett had no specific assigned duty post but was free to position himself wherever he felt most needed. If there is no evidence to suggest that Crockett was assigned to defend the palisade, where did he die? There are only two nineteenth century accounts that identify where his body was found after the battle. In 1860, Francisco Ruiz, the alcalde of San Antonio during the 1836 siege, said: "Toward the west and in the small fort opposite the city, we found the body of Colonel Crockett."[10] Susannah Hannig (the former Mrs. Dickinson, wife of Alamo defender Almeron Dickinson) stated in 1875: "I recognized Col. Crockett lying dead and mutilated between the church and the two story barrack building, and even remember seeing his peculiar cap lying by his side."[11]

There is another account, by Andrea Castanon de Vallanueva (Madam Candelaria), which purports to describe Crockett's death and where it occurred. According to her account, given in an interview to William Corner in 1888, "David Crockett . . . advanced from the Church building 'towards the wall or rampart running from the end of the stockade, . . . when suddenly a volley was fired by the Mexicans causing him to fall forward on his face, dead.'"[12] This was one of several accounts she gave of Crockett's death, none of which agree in the slightest. Madam Candelaria claimed to have been Col. James Bowie's nurse during the siege of the Alamo. It is doubtful that she was actually present during the thirteen-day siege, and the various accounts she gave were too conflicting to be considered reliable, even if she was there.

In the end, we have two seemingly contradictory stories of where Crockett died: one by Ruiz and the other by Hannig. In *Eyewitness to the Alamo*, author Bill Groneman raises the possibility that both Ruiz and Hannig may actually have described the same location. Ruiz's description of "the small fort opposite the city" in which Crockett's body was found, could be that of the area directly outside of the front (the west) of the Alamo church. This courtyard was opposite a small section of San Antonio known as La Villita, situated on the same side of the San Antonio River as the Alamo. LaVillita may have been mistranslated or misinterpreted as 'the city.'"[13]

Since the area in front of the church is enclosed on all sides (by the church, the palisade, the low wall between the Long Barracks and the Low Barracks, the two-story hospital and the south wall of the convent yard), then it could be described as a "small fort." However, it is more likely that Ruiz's statement was interpreted correctly and should indicate the area along the west wall of the main plaza. This is especially true since he correctly described the locations of Travis' body "on the north battery of the fortress" and of Bowie's body "in one of the rooms of the south side."[14]

If the accounts by Ruiz and Hannig describe different locations, then a choice has to be made between them. This requires an evaluation of the circumstances in which each statement was made. Susannah Hannig's story was given in an interview to James M. Morphis who was writing a book on the history of Texas. It is written as a first-person narrative but the words almost certainly come from Morphis. It was taken from an interview and there is no way of knowing what questions she was responding to. She gave information on the deaths of Bowie, Travis, and Bonham that could not have had previous knowledge of. And her account contains at least one error: she said that the body of Colonel Travis "lay on top of the church."[15] In a later interview, when questioned on Colonel Crockett's death, it was stated: "He was killed, she believes."[16]

Any evaluation of Hannig's statement must consider her emotional state at the time when she said she saw Crockett's body. She had lost her husband in battle, saw at least one person (possibly several) brutally murdered in front of her, and was herself shot in the leg. She was quickly hurried from the compound, so any glimpse she had of Crockett's body would, of necessity, have been fleeting.[17]

The account of Ruiz was translated from his written statement. Rather than an interview, it is in his own words—although there is the possibility of a mistranslation or misinterpretation.

And since the original no longer exists, there is no means of verification. Ruiz was asked by Santa Anna specifically to locate and identify the bodies of Travis, Bowie, and Crockett, so he was given free access to the Alamo's grounds to look for them. Seeing the terrible carnage and torn bodies, many of them friends and neighbors, would have caused an immense strain; however, it would have been nothing compared to that which Susannah Dickinson would have been subjected to. His account is straightforward and unembellished. Taking everything into consideration, the statement of Francisco Ruiz has to be preferred.

If the account of Ruiz is correct and Crockett's body was found "toward the west" and in "the small fort opposite the city," where exactly was the "small fort?" C. J. Long located the small fort in the area near the Alamo headquarters where the carronade (or gunade) was located.[18] Bounded on the west by the West Wall, on the south by the artillery command post or the southwest gun platform, on the east by the acequia and on the north by the headquarters building, this area could be described as a "small fort." However, there was another area along the West Wall that better fits this description.

The plan of the Alamo by José Juan Sanchez Navarro shows three semicircular outer defense works. These occur at the North Wall (in front of the Fortin de Teran battery where Travis died) at the southwest corner of the West Wall, and at the area of the West Wall just to the north of the gunnade and outside the Alamo headquarters. Navarro's map key describes these outerworks as "circular saps with a moat and stockade defending the exterior of the enclosure."[19]

In Stephen L. Hardin's *Texian Iliad: A Military History of the Texas Revolution, 1835-1836*, artist Gary S. Zaboly depicts the outerwork along the West Wall in a plan of the Alamo and describes it as a "semicircular palisade and narrow trench." Zaboly believes this area would have served as a bastion to provide enfilading fire at any enemy troops who reached the West Wall.[20] Access to this area would probably have been through the window in the outside wall of the Alamo headquarters. This outerwork better fits Ruiz's description of a "small fort" than the area inside the wall near the gun platform where the gunade was located.

If David Crockett was killed in the small outerwork along the West Wall, is there any way one can determine how he died? His death by execution can be discounted. Since Santa Anna asked at least three people—Joe,[21] Ruiz and Ramon Musquiz[22]—to find the former Tennessee congressman's body, there is little chance that Crockett was one of the men executed on his orders. If he ordered him killed, why would he have needed to have him identified?

There is no way to know exactly how Crockett died but certain possibilities can be explored. The light infantry of Col. Juan Morales that attacked the South Wall was forced to veer to the west where they took cover in some ruined *jacales* to the west and southwest of the Alamo. From this cover, they sniped at the Alamo defenders along the West Wall. There is a possibility that Crockett was killed during this desultory fire.

A stronger possibility is that Crockett was killed when the outwork he defended was overrun by troops under the command of either Gen. Martin Perfecto de Cos or Colonel Morales. This is supported by an account attributed to Travis' slave, Joe, who was directed to identify Crockett's body after the battle. According to this account, "David Crockett, and a few of the devoted friends who entered the fort with him, were found lying together, with twenty-one of the slain enemy around them."[23] This would suggest that Crockett and those with him died desperately in an attempt to defend the bastion against the assaulting infantry.

In summation, the evidence that David Crockett was killed in the courtyard in front of the church is insubstantial since it is based only on Susannah Dickinson's testimony. The possibility that he was killed in a "small fort" along the West Wall is also supported by only one account—that of Francisco Ruiz. However, the circumstances under which Ruiz's account was provided, and the conditions under which he identified Crockett's body, make his version the preferable one of the two. The small circular bastion that projected outside the West Wall to provide a wider firing range better fits Ruiz's description of the "small fort" than any other location in the Alamo.

Notes

1. Ernest Hemingway, ed. *Men at War* (New York, 1958), 167.
2. John Myers Myers, *The Alamo* (Lincoln, NE, 1973), 223.
3. Lon Tinkle, *13 Days to Glory* (College Station, TX, 1985), 213.
4. Walter Lord, *A Time to Stand* (New York, 1961), 161.
5. Dr. John Sutherland, *The Fall of the Alamo* (San Antonio, TX, 1936), 20.
6. Bill Groneman, Alamo Defenders (Austin, TX, 1990) 22, 26-28, 58.
7. Sutherland, 11-12
8. Thomas Ricks Lindley, *The Revealing of Dr. John Sutherland* (Austin, TX; private paper, 1989), 1-34.
9. Wallace O. Chariton, *100 Days in Texas; The Alamo Letters* (Plano, TX, 1990), 271.
10. Timothy Matovina, *The Alamo Remembered; Tejano Accounts and Perspectives* (Austin, TX, 1995), 44.
11. Bill Groneman, *Eyewitness to the Alamo* (Plano, TX, 1996), 69-70.
12. *Ibid.*, 109.
13. *Ibid.*, 60.
14. Matovina, 44
15. Groneman, *Eyewitness to the Alamo* (Plano, TX, 1996), 69-70.
16. Ibid., 74.
17. *Ibid.*, 23, 69, 73-74, 78, 174.
18. C. J. Long, 1836; *The Alamo* (San Antonio, TX, 1981), 5, 9-10.
19. Helen Hunnicutt, "A Mexican View of the Texas War: Memoirs of a Veteran of the Two Battles of the Alamo," *The Library Chronicles of the University of Texas*, Vol. IV, No. 2, 72-73.
20. Stephen L. Hardin, *Texian Iliad; A Military History of the Texas Revolution, 1835-1836* (Austin, TX, 1994), 112, 114.
21. Groneman: *Eyewitness*, 52. This account (Edward Stiff's "The Texan Immigrant") is attributed to Santa Anna's servant, Ben. It states that he "was taken to the fort to designate their bodies (Crockett, Bowie and Travis) . . . and found no less than 16 dead Mexicans around the corpse of Colonel Crockett and one across it with the huge knife of Davy buried in the Mexican's bosom to the hilt." Groneman states: "It sounds more likely that Stiff may have been confusing Ben's accounts with one of those of Joe."
22. Matovina, 37.
23. Groneman, *Eyewitness*, 26.

"Crockett & Russel" by John Bourdage, Alamo Journal, no. 86 (May 1993).

Davy Crockett: A Hero for All Decades

by William R. Chemerka

Of all the Alamo heroes, none have achieved the legendary status of Davy Crockett. Even before he died at the famous mission–fortress on March 6, 1836, Crockett was a celebrated political figure in the United States. In fact, the three-term congressman's popularity was unrivaled in the mid-1830s. His 1834 autobiography, *A Narrative of the Life of David Crockett of the State of Tennessee*, was incredibly successful. Several printings of the homespun literature classic were published in the book's first year alone. A year later, two ghostwritten books, *Col. Crockett's Tour to the North and Down East, and the Life of Martin Van Buren*, were published.

The first of the lively Crockett almanacs also debuted in 1835 and built upon the image created in the well-received 1831 stage play *The Lion of the West*, which featured a Crockett-like character, Nimrod Wildfire, as its lead. In addition, hundreds of newspaper accounts of Crockett's frontier and congressional exploits entertained readers throughout the nation. And in 1835, Crockett was also celebrated in song, courtesy of "Go Ahead," a march dedicated to Colonel Crockett.

After his death, Davy Crockett became even a larger figure in popular culture. Of course, the Walt Disney-produced *Davy Crockett, King of the Wild Frontier* phenomenon of the 1950s was the high point of the Crockett legend. However, surprisingly enough, every decade since his death, Crockett has remained in the public's collective consciousness. As a matter of fact, the time period 1836 (from Crockett's death) to 1953 (the year before the debut of Disney's *Davy Crockett, Indian Fighter*) is consistently rich with Crockett myth and lore.

The legend of Davy Crockett was established in 1836 when Richard Penn Smith penned *Col. Crockett's Exploits and Adventures in Texas*. The book was supposedly an autobiography that covered his entire life. There's even a final entry on March 6, 1836, which Crockett "wrote" during the battle of the Alamo!

The most enduring aspect of the Crockett legend in the nineteenth century was the publication of the Crockett almanacs. These glorified farmers' almanacs were printed regularly until 1856. The titles of these innocuous pamphlets were animated and inviting, like 1839's *The Crockett Almanac: Containing Adventures, Exploits, Sprees & Scrapes in the West, & Life and Manners in the Backwoods*. But the almanac's contents were even more outrageous. Crockett is depicted taming all sorts of wild animals (especially bears), riding up Niagara Falls on an alligator and battling comets! The 1837 Almanack described his death at the Alamo with particular exaggeration: "It was calculated that during the siege he killed no less than 85 men, and wounded 120 besides, as he was one of the best shooters of the west, and he had four rifles, with two men to load constantly, and he fired as fast as they could load, nearly always hitting his man."

Crockett's musical legacy continued in 1837 with *Crockett's Free and Easy Songbook*, and in 1839, *Colonel Crockett: A Virginia Reel* was published. A new edition of *Crockett's Free and Easy Songbook* was printed in 1846.

There was even a 19th century transportation legacy associated with Crockett. A British-made steam locomotive, the *Davy Crockett*, began operations in 1833 on the Saratoga and Schenectady Railroad in New York State. However, the most important vehicle was the clipper ship *David Crockett*. The 1,679-ton craft was launched on October 18, 1853, from Mystic, Connecticut, and for the next nearly forty years the grand sailing vessel traveled the New York-to-Liverpool and New York-to-San Francisco routes. The ship's gorgeous figurehead was never mounted on the bow; instead, it carefully rested on the deck.

April 12, 1861, brought the issue of civil war to the United States. To be sure, during the War Between the States, Crockett's legend was overshadowed by the exploits of such individuals as Robert E. Lee, Ulysses S. Grant, Thomas "Stonewall" Jackson, and William T. Sherman, to name an obvious few. Nevertheless, Crockett remained in print thanks to the Beadle's Dime Biographical Library that published *Col. David Crockett, The Celebrated Hunter, Wit and Patriot* in 1861, and the *Life and Adventures of Colonel David Crockett* in 1864. During the last year of the war, *Life of Crockett*, a reissue of a previous "autobiography," was published by Philadelphia's John E. Potter.

Following the Civil War, Crockett was introduced to yet another generation of Americans courtesy of new periodical articles and dramatic stage productions. An April 1867 *Harper's New Monthly Magazine* featured a six-page story titled "Davy Crockett's Electioneering Tour," and the play *Davy Crockett; or, Be Sure You're Right, Then Go Ahead* debuted in Rochester, New York, on September 23, 1872. Penned by Frank Hitchcock Murdock and Frank Mayo, who played the title role, the play depicted Crockett as a fearful frontier hero who maintains a ramrod-straight moral posture and wins the girl before the curtain falls. The popular production ran until 1896 when its star, Frank Mayo, died.

Despite the long-term run of the Murdock-Mayo collaboration, the printed page served as the primary cultural medium in reinforcing the legend of the famous backwoods congressman. Edward S. Ellis (who sometimes used the pen name Charles E. LaSalle) was the nineteenth century's most prolific Crockett author. Ellis, who wrote titles for both adults and young readers, created such works as: *The Texas Trailer, or, Davy Crockett's Last Bear Hunt* in 1871; *The Bear-Hunter, or, Davy Crockett as a Spy* in 1873; *Sockdolager! A Tale of Davy Crockett, in which the Old Tennessee Bear Hunter Meets up with the Constitution of the United States* in 1876; *Colonel Crockett, the Texan Trailer* (a reprint of the 1871 title) in 1878; *The Life of Colonel David Crockett* in 1884; and *Col. Crockett, the Bear King* in 1886. John S. C. Abbott wrote *David Crockett: His Life and Adventures* in 1874 for Dodd, Mead and Company's "American Pioneers and Patriots" series. Abbott said that "there is probably not an adult American, in all these widespread States, who has not heard of David Crockett." A year later on the eve of the American Centennial, George Cary Eggleston penned the biography *David Crockett*.

In 1883, Crockett was included in an article in the *Magazine of American History* and in 1886 Kit Clyde's "dime novel," *Davy Crockett's Vow, or, His Last Shot for Vengeance*, was published. William F. Cody's *Story of the Wild West* in 1888 included Crockett along with other legendary frontier heroes.

America, of course, became increasingly industrial in the late nineteenth century. Captains of industry like John D. Rockefeller, J. P. Morgan, and Andrew Carnegie dominated the economic horizon of the approaching twentieth century. And a tidal wave of immigration, technological developments, transportation improvements, and urbanization was reshaping the American landscape. Increasingly, Crockett's frontier was becoming the "Old West." According to historian Frederick Jackson Turner in his seminal 1893 Chicago address, the ever-changing frontier had created and maintained America's democratic and egalitarian character. He carefully described the first "moving mass" of settlers into the Piedmont region, which included "the ancestors of John C. Calhoun, Abraham Lincoln, Jefferson Davis, Stonewall Jackson, James K. Polk, Sam Houston, and Davy Crockett...."

During the final decade of the nineteenth century, Turner's frontier had closed. Still, the public's interest in the frontier remained strong. To satisfy the public's demand, Buffalo Bill's Wild West shows and printed stories about George Custer, Annie Oakley, cowboy shoot-em-ups, and the legend of Davy Crockett helped keep the spirit of the frontier alive.

By 1898, America became a world power. Its imperialistic victory in the Spanish American War spawned a new cadre of heroes, from Commodore George Dewey to Theodore Roosevelt. But the legend of Davy Crockett remained in the public arena as new books sprang from the presses.

In 1900, Frances M. Perry penned *The Story of David Crockett For Young Readers*, a title in the Baldwin's Biographical Booklet series. The new century witnessed the *The Life of David Crockett* in 1902, essentially a combined reprint of his autobiography and his ghostwritten Texas exploits. In 1905, Harriet G. Reiter wrote *David Crockett*, a 31-page booklet in the Instructor Literature Series. Reiter's Crockett "stood alone like a lion at bay" in the final moments of her description of the famous frontiersman at the Alamo. In 1908, Edward Willett wrote *Davy Crockett's Boy Hunter*, a pulp reader in the popular Beadles Frontier Series, and Everett McNeil wrote *In Texas With Davy Crockett; A Story of the Texas War of Independence*.

The embryonic world of cinema spawned the first celluloid tribute to the legendary Alamo hero in a 1909 silent film titled *Davy Crockett—in Hearts United*, which starred Charles K. French. Another silent film, simply called *Davy Crockett*, was released the next year. Crockett's character appeared in the 1911 film *The Immortal Alamo*, and in 1915 A. D. Sears had the featured role in *The Martyrs of the Alamo*. A year later, Dustin Farnum was the frontier character in yet another film titled *Davy Crockett*.

In the 1920s several songs titled "Davy Crockett" were published and Sunset Productions released the silent film *Davy Crockett at the Fall of the Alamo* in 1926 with Cullen Landis in the title role. The decade began with a feature story on Crockett in the February 1920 issue of *The Mentor: Pioneers of the Great West*. In 1921, Yale University Press published the multivolume The Chronicles of America Series. Volume 24 of the series, *Texas and the Mexican War*, featured Homeric-like passages on the legendary backwoodsman: "David Crockett, who had come from his native Tennessee to throw in his lot with the Texans, sold his life amid the last massacre as grimly as a Norse Viking in an Icelandic saga."

Years before the Crockett marketing craze of the 1950s, various enterprises exploited the coonskin congressman's image in the 1920s. Southern Pacific Railroad, for example, used Crockett's impression to promote its passenger service. In 1928, the Boston-based John Hancock Insurance Company produced a sixteen-page booklet titled *David Crockett: Backwoodsman and Congressman*. The booklet stated: "We do not know how Davy Crockett died. Some think that he was among the last six survivors, that they surrendered and were taken before Santa Anna, who ordered that they be killed at once. But it is more probable that the brave woodsman died with his face to the foe, undaunted and resolute—on his lips, the words, 'Go Ahead.'" The decade ended with a Crockett cover story ("Davy Crockett, Hero and Congressman") in the May 1929 issue of *Frontier Times*, the publication that was "devoted to frontier history, border tragedy and pioneer achievements."

The 1930s was a decade rich in Crockett media. In 1931, the New York-based Conqueror Records released vocalist Chubby Parker's "Davey Crockett." Constance Rourke's 1934 book *Davy Crockett* was a unique volume, combining storytelling with an interesting final chapter of the Crockett almanacs. Rourke was quite accurate when she stated: "About no single American figure have so many legends clustered."

Lane Chandler played the famous frontiersman in Columbia Pictures' *Heroes of the Alamo* in 1937. Said film historian Frank Thompson of Chandlers' performance: "Crockett is younger than he should be, but otherwise is a canny mixture of the historical and the legendary." In 1938, Sterling Waters starred as Crockett in the narrated educational film *The Alamo: "Shrine of Texas Liberty."* A year later, Robert Barratt portrayed Crockett in the Sam Houston bio pic, *Man of Conquest*, which starred Richard Dix. Surprisingly, Barratt's Crockett is killed with a pistol in the film. Also in 1939, Richard M. Dorson edited selections from the lively nineteenth century Crockett almanacs and published them as *Davy Crockett: American Comic Legend*.

The 1940s continued the Crockett legacy as writers supplied the public's demand for material about the famous Alamo defender. For example, Frank Beals' *Davy Crockett* was published in 1941 as part of the Chicago-based Wheeler Publishing Company's "American Adventure Series." Also in 1941, Crockett appeared in the comic book *World Famous Heroes*, no. 1.

To be sure, news of World War II dominated the readings of Americans between late 1941 and 1945, but that did not stop writers and publishers from delivering articles about Davy Crockett. In 1943, for instance, the April issue of *Encore* magazine featured an eleven-page article titled "Davy Crockett—The Siege of the Alamo." A year later, Irwin Shapiro wrote *Yankee Thunder: The Legendary Life of Davy Crockett* and Walter Blair devoted a chapter to Crockett in his book *Tall Tale America*.

Following the war in 1948, Crockett appeared at the Alamo in the comic book *Dead-Eye Western Comics*, no. 1. In 1949,

Aileen W. Parks authored *Davy Crockett, Young Rifleman*, and Crockett appeared in Commended Comics' *Tex Granger*, issue no. 20.

The early 1950s were filled with images and stories of Davy Crockett. In fact, the decade began with a Crockett film, *Davy Crockett—Indian Scout*. Although the Lew Landers-directed motion picture starred George Montgomery as a cousin to the famous Davy Crockett, it nevertheless maintained the popular-culture tradition of acknowledging the frontier hero. Crockett was illustrated by artist Benton Clark on the cover of *Blue Book Magazine of Adventure in Fact and Fiction* in June 1951. The magazine included a story titled "Men of America—David Crockett." Furthermore, Avon Comics produced a single title called *Frontier Fighter Davy Crockett* in 1951. And the famous backwoodsman was featured in *Indian Fighter*, no. 6, also in 1951. Among the best books for young readers was Enid Lamonte Meadowcraft's *The Story of Davy Crockett*, published in 1952. Meadowcraft traced Crockett's life from his boyhood years to his death at the Alamo.

However, Walt Disney's Davy Crockett production dwarfs every previous popular-culture effort. The three chronologically-arranged, hour-long episodes became television's first mini-series in the 1954-55 season. Starring Texas-born actor Fess Parker, the Disney series traced Crockett's adult life from the Creek Indian War in 1813 to his death at the Alamo in 1836.

From the conclusion of the first episode, "Davy Crockett, Indian Fighter," on December 15, 1954, Disney realized that he had a huge hit on his hands, especially the episode's signature theme song, "The Ballad of Davy Crockett." The tune was covered by numerous artists, including Gabe Drake and the Woodsmen, Walter Schumann, Tex Ritter, Mitch Miller, Tennessee Ernie Ford, and Burl Ives, among others. One version on Cadence Records sung by Bill Hayes sold several million copies and topped the national record charts for five consecutive weeks. Even Fess Parker's version of the song sold a million copies and reached #5 on the charts.

On January 26, 1955, "Davy Crockett Goes to Congress" was broadcast on the nation's small screens. Although targeted to an elementary school-age audience, Disney took particular care to make it as historically correct as possible. "We filmed the

Congress scenes at the Nashville, Tennessee state house, and we actually used Andrew Jackson's home, The Hermitage, in the exterior shots," said Parker in a November 1987 interview in *The Alamo Journal*.

On February 23, "Davy Crockett at the Alamo" aired. The episode's ending, which inspired a generation of youngsters around the nation to restage their own Battle of the Alamo in backyards and city streets, is a classic. Crockett, depicted as the last defender, swings his rifle back and forth as Mexican soldiers climb the stairs and walls. Crockett is not shown dying; instead, the camera closes in on him as his inevitable fate approaches. "There was a concern by Disney to take into account both history and the feelings of the kids," said Parker in *The Alamo Journal* interview. "The final scene was definitely under-rehearsed. We had stunt men and stunt extras working in the scene, and there was a considerable amount of uncertain footing, especially where I was swinging my rifle back and forth." The ending's last shot is of the modern flag of Texas, which dissolves into the final page of Crockett's journal. Of all the Crockett and Alamo films, it is Fess Parker's image of Crockett swinging his rifle in a final act of supreme courage that remains most memorable of all. Disney repeated the three episodes on April 13, April 27, and May 11.

America's youngsters reacted to Fess Parker's portrayal of Davy Crockett with a collective frenzy. The April 25, 1955, issue of *Life* magazine chronicled the growing Davy Crockett craze with a vivid seven-page spread. *Life* reported that "raccoon tails used to sell for 2-cents apiece, but with the shrill demand for coonskin hats, the market soared to 8-cents, and now it has become an open question which will be exhausted first: the supply of raccoons or the parents who have to buy the caps." However, the demand for coonskin caps became so great that raccoon tails increased in price to $5 each!

Davy Crockett merchandise filled the store shelves and the baby boomers purchased the items with glee. Disney marketed a few hundred items under the "Walt Disney's official Davy Crockett, King of the Wild Frontier" logo. In fact, Disney's agreement with various manufacturers left no doubt that his merchandise was not even to be associated with non-Disney Crockett items. One contractual demand noted that certain display items were "for use only with the display and promotion of Davy Crockett (Fess Parker) Official Walt Disney designs and products produced only by manufacturers authorized and licensed by Walt Disney Productions." Disney's numerous Crockett goods ranged from games, guitars, and pencil cases—to puzzles, bubble gum cards, clothing, and of course, coonskin caps.

The Crockett craze was chronicled by a host of magazines, including front-page cover stories in *TV Guide* and *Look*.

Disney kept up the Crockett interest by releasing an edited theatrical version of the three TV episodes for movie audiences in May of 1955. Fess Parker and Walt Disney appeared on the cover of *Look* magazine on July 26, 1955.

In early August, Republic Pictures released *The Last Command*, an Alamo movie that starred Arthur Hunnicutt as a bearded and buckskinned Crockett. *Alamo Movies* author, Frank Thompson, said of Hunnicutt: "Most movie Crocketts have, inexplicably, tended to concentrate on the sober side of the man. Hunnicutt gives a good speech, and knows how to get a laugh. Best of all, he isn't overly heroic."

During the summer of 1955, Disney filmed new television episodes for the 1955-56 season that described events in Crockett's life before his fateful encounter at the Alamo. "Davy Crockett's Keelboat Race" aired on November 16, 1955, and "Davy Crockett and the River Pirates" was broadcast on December 14, 1955. Both episodes, essentially the first "prequels" in television history, were repeated in January and February of 1956. And like the first three episodes, both were edited and released as a feature film, *Davy Crockett and the River Pirates*.

Disney didn't have a monopoly on Crockett's image—only Fess Parker's image of Crockett. Since Crockett was a historical character, he was marketed generically by hundreds of manufacturers. Thousands of objects were manufactured. Crockett clothing, curtains, rugs, lunch boxes, pin-back buttons, glasses, cookies and cookie jars, plastic trains, lamps, furniture, rings, rubber knives, toy guns—and coonskin caps—flooded the market. *Time* magazine estimated that approximately $100 million worth of Crockett merchandise was sold during the first quarter of 1955 alone. When the craze subsided in 1956, some $300 million worth of items had been sold.

Amidst all of the toys and games during the Crockett craze came James Shackford's excellent book *David Crockett: The Man and the Legend* in 1956. Shackford's superior work was augmented by dozens of other authors and publishers. Children's books in particular were popular, to say nothing of the various Davy Crockett comic books. Among the best books were: Ardis Edwards Burton's *Legends of Davy Crockett*, Bruce Grant's *Davy Crockett: American Hero*, Felix Hutton's *The Picture Story of Davy Crockett* and Irwin Shapiro's *Walt Disney's Davy Crockett, King of the Wild Frontier*. Disney briefly revived interest in Crockett when he kicked off the 1958-59 *Disneyland* television season with a rebroadcast of the original three episodes.

No one could top Disney's Crockett, but one man tried. In 1960 John Wayne released his epic film, *The Alamo*, in which he starred as Davy Crockett. Wayne's Crockett was a larger-than-life character who was quick with his fists and respectful of the ladies. Fess Parker's characterization covered Crockett's life from 1813 to 1836; Wayne's interpretation covered the last weeks of the frontiersman's life. Yet in those weeks—even during the siege of the Alamo—Wayne's Crockett blows up a Mexican cannon, rustles a herd of Santa Anna's cattle and wears the most diverse wardrobe in celluloid frontier history.

In 1961, Anne Ford wrote the children's book *Davy Crockett: A See and Read Biography*. During the mid-sixties, additional songs were recorded about Crockett. Even Disney attempted a Crockett revival of sorts when the three episodes were rebroadcast to start the 1963-64 television season's debut of *Walt Disney's Wonderful World of Color* on three consecutive weeks beginning September 8, 1963. In fact, Disney took out a full-page ad in *Billboard* magazine and heralded the Crockett craze of the previous decade. Stated the ad: "Remember? 1955. Davy Crockett took the nation by storm. 10,000,000 single records were sold! 750,000 albums were sold!"

During the 1970s, the 1837 *Crockett Almanack* was reprinted by the Huntington Library and Art Gallery, Richard M. Dorson's edited *Davy Crockett: American Comic Legend* was re-released and Dee Hicks recorded the song "Davy Crockett." Davy Crockett even appeared in a 1971 episode of *You Are There*, a program that brought viewers back to the past. In 1975, Carmen Perry's translation of the José Enrique de la Peña papers stated that Crockett survived the Battle of the Alamo, was captured and executed. Dan Kilgore's controversial 1978 book, *How Did Davy Die?*, supported Perry's allegation and ushered in an era of debate on Crockett's death.

A Crockett renaissance of sorts emerged in the 1980s. The decade marked the bicentennial of the famous frontiersman's birth, and the Texas Sesquicentennial in 1986. Celebrations were held at Crockett's birthplace in Tennessee, and in San Antonio, Texas. At dawn on March 6, 1986, coonskin cap-wearing baby boomers descended on Alamo Plaza to salute their fallen hero and his Alamo comrades in arms.

In the 1980s the Disney studio produced a new Davy Crockett series for television, starring Tim Dunigan in the title role, and Walt Disney's *Davy Crockett, King of the Wild Frontier*, was released on videocassette. *Texas Monthly* featured a cover story titled "Davy Crockett, Still King of the Wild Frontier" by Paul Andrew Hutton. The magazine also featured an interview with Fess Parker.

James Shackford's definitive biography, *David Crockett: The Man and the Legend*, was also reprinted in 1986 by the University of North Carolina Press. The best book of the decade was *Crockett at Two Hundred; New Perspectives on the Man and the Myth*, which was carefully edited in 1989 by Michael A. Lofaro and Joe Cummings. Other notable books included Richard Boyd Hauck's *Crockett: A Bio-Bibliography* and a University of Nebraska Press release of Crockett's 1834 autobiography with a lively and informative introduction by Paul Andrew Hutton. Gary Foreman wrote *Crockett: The Gentleman from the Cane—A Comprehensive View of the Folkhero Americans Thought They Knew*. The glossy booklet vividly reflected the Crockett of history and the Crockett of popular culture.

Davy Crockett appeared on the cover of *The Alamo Journal* for the first time in 1987. Artists such as Joseph Musso, Robert Weil, Gary Zaboly, John Bourdage, and Howard Bender have contributed skillful views of the Crockett of history and the Crockett of popular culture for the quarterly. And since its inception, the publication has examined every facet of his legend. The debate over the death of Crockett was carried in the pages of *The Alamo Journal* thanks to a series of provocative essays penned by Dr. James E. Crisp and Thomas Ricks Lindley.

In the 1990s more Crockett titles appeared than any other time except the 1950s. Bill Groneman countered Dan Gilgore and other de la Peña supporters with *Defense of a Legend*; Disney Press released a half-dozen new Crockett books for young readers; Mark Derr penned *The Frontiersman: The Real Life and the Many Legends of Davy Crockett*; and Paul Anderson chronicled *The Davy Crockett Craze*. Jeff Long trashed the "king of the wild frontier" in *Duel of Eagles*; Cameron Judd created a lusty fictionalized frontiersman in *Crockett of Tennessee*; and noted Civil War historian William C. Davis traced Crockett's life in 1998 with his comprehensive *Three Roads to the Alamo*. Western writer David Thompson wrote eight fictional tales about Crockett in 1997 and 1998, including *Mississippi Mayhem, Comanche Country*, and *Texican Terror*. Bill Groneman explored the controversy of Crockett's final moments in the 1999 book *Death of a Legend*.

This writer penned *The Davy Crockett Almanac & Book of Lists* in 2000. The book was a compilation of nearly everything written on the famous frontier hero—from his exploits in the Creek Indian War, Congress and the Texas War for Independence to his enduring status as a cultural icon over the centuries. The book raised several fundamental questions about Crockett. For example, was he the animated "half-horse, half-alligator" character as described in contemporary literature or merely an inarticulate representative of poor canebrake squatters who, like him, saw the Western horizon as a place of economic opportunity? Was Crockett a self-promoting politician or a genuine democrat who fought for those citizens who lacked a voice in government?

The story of Davy Crockett became part of the twenty-first century when The History Channel aired *Boone and Crockett: The Hunter Heroes* during the summer of 2001. The two-hour documentary, written by Paul A. Hutton and Dan Gagliasso and directed by Crockett author Gary Foreman (*The Gentleman from the Cane; A Comprehensive View of the Folkhero Americans Thought They Knew*), compared and contrasted the lives of America's most well-known frontier personalities. The Crockett of this documentary (portrayed by Mark Baker) was depicted as an adventurous, honest and likable man.

Also in 2001, the Walt Disney company rereleased the five original television episodes of *Davy Crockett, King of the Wild Frontier* on DVD. And Fess Parker, renewed his "Talkin' With Fess" column in *The Alamo Journal*.

The new century continued to salute Davy Crockett in a most appropriate way. A large exhibit on Crockett debuted on March 2, 2002, at the Bob Bullock Texas State History Museum in Austin, Texas. Titled "Sunrise in His Pocket: The Life. Legend and Legacy of Davy Crockett," the extensive exhibit traced Crockett's life through original artifacts, letters, almanacs, art, antique toys, collectibles, and other items. The museum augmented its display with "Davy Crockett in Texas," a live storytelling performance.

Billy Bob Thornton became the newest celluloid Crockett when he portrayed the famous Tennessean in the John Lee Hancock-directed *The Alamo* in 2004. The motion picture was a disappointment at the box office, but Thornton's performance was memorable thanks to the actor's meticulous creation of a unique historical character who struggled with the conflicting identities of his public ad personal life.

In 2003, *The Crockett Chronicle*, a quarterly dedicated to the life and legend of David Crackett, made its debut.

Clearly, the legend of Davy Crockett is alive and well in yet another decade. May we always continue in our lives with Crockett's motto in mind: "Be sure you're right, then go ahead."

$5.00 ISSUE #126 SEPT. 2002

THE ALAMO JOURNAL

The Official Publication of THE ALAMO SOCIETY

"Mexican Regular, 1829" by Gary Zaboly, Alamo Journal, no. 126 (Sept. 2002).

Latest from Texas

by Robert L. Durham

POSTSCRIPT—We stop the Press to announce the fall of Bexar, and the slaughter of 187 brave fellows, principally Americans, who were fighting for the constitution of Texas. The Mexican army was headed by Santa Anna in person, which numbered 8000 strong, and which succeeded, after loosing [sic] 6 or 700 men, in surrounding the garrison. After all were slain but seven, within its walls, the remaining Americans offered to surrender, among whom was Davy Crockett, and it is said that when there was no quarter shown, he fought like a tiger until he fell covered with wounds. The gallant commander, Col. Travis, before he would suffer himself to be taken alive, drew a pistol from his belt and put an end to his existence by lodging its contents in his own head.[1]

The above quote, from an Ohio newspaper dated 16 April 1836, over a month after the fall of the Alamo on 6 March, illustrates how long it took the news to travel in 1836. Prior to the wire services of Associated Press and United Press International, the only way for a local newspaper to receive international news was by picking up stories from larger papers they subscribed to. This article is a view of the Texas Revolution as seen through the pages of small town Ohio newspapers of the period. Despite many inaccuracies and exaggerations in these stories, they allowed people to follow the war from beginning to end.

Amazingly, even before the revolution began, volunteers from the United States started mobilizing to lend a hand. The following short article, written prior to the Battle of Gonzales, tried to discourage young men from heading off to Texas:

> When we see the sons of the West, or the sons of any other part of the Union, marching to a foreign country to maintain by force and arms the principles of '76, we shall think they have very little to do at home.[2]

Once the war began in earnest, the same newspaper encouraged volunteers to go to Texas. Interestingly, the following article responds to an early example of propaganda, that the Mexicans were inciting the Indians to attack the Texians:

> Americans to the rescue! Remember the condition of our revolutionary ancestors, when the Indians were excited against them! Shall we suffer our colonial friends to [be] massacred by Indians hired by Mexicans, and have them driven from the colonies, which they have honorably purchased and laboriously improved?[3]

By early December 1835, more information had been received, gleaned from the *New Orleans Union*, the *New Orleans True American*, the *Louisville Journal*, and others, that "several skirmishes had taken place which had resulted uniformly in favor of the Texians."[4]

They also amended an earlier story, adding new inaccuracies, when they learned that the "report that was prevalent some weeks ago, that the Comanche Indians would join the Mexican forces is totally unfounded, for an engagement had also taken place between the Indians and Mexican soldiers and like many great battles we read of in modern history, victory was claimed on both sides. Be this as it may, our informant says that he saw on the field of battle several dead horses and Indians."[5]

The local newspapers also had more details on the buildup of Texian troops for the siege of Bexar:

> Gen. Houston left San Felippe [sic—Felipe] about the 22d ult., with a considerable reinforcement of troops, to join the commander in chief, Austin, near San Antonio. Our informant also states that he met a company of 80 men from the neighbor-

hood of Nacogdoches; another of 33, and another of 25 from the same settlement; and the company of about 60 which went from this place, who were to be joined at Nacogdoches by an additional corps—all of whom were in high health and spirits, and marching on to San Antonio. A fine cavalry company of sixteen men, from the neighborhood of Natchez, were also met on their way . . .

POSTSCRIPT.—A letter just received from General Austin, dated the 20th instant, informs us that a division of the army had advanced and taken up a position at Salado, within five miles of San Antonio, in doing which they had come in contact with an advanced guard of the enemy, who still continues in sight, on the hill between our troops, and San Antonio. General Austin continues to urge reinforcements to hasten as fast as possible.[6]

The advance guard of the Texian forces moving against Bexar met a body of Mexican troops at Mission Concepción on 28 October 1835:

LATEST FROM TEXAS.—Intelligence was received yesterday from the camp of the Texians near Bexar, dated 1st inst. that an engagement had occurred between the Mexicans and the Texians. The former were to the number of 300 cavalry, and 100 infantry; and attacked the latter in their encampment under Colonel Bowie and Captain Fanning [sic], with a force of 90 men, but the Texians repulsed the attack with only the loss of one man, while 16 were killed and as many wounded on the part of the assailants . . . The main body of the Texians shortly advanced; and the enemy retreated to the garrison of San Antonio.[7]

STILL LATER.—We learn from a gentleman that has just arrived, by land from Texas, that the Texians had been able to surround General Coss [sic] and his small army of 700 men, and that all chance of escape was shut out from him. The Texians speak confidently of an easy victory.[8]

In addition to news from Texas, local U.S. newspapers also received news from Mexico, which they duly reported. We find that Mexico was already preparing to send reinforcements to Texas: "We learn that an expedition had been fitted out at Vera

Cruz, to proceed against Texas . . . St. Ana [sic] was to have set out for Mexico on the 9th, to proceed thence, as was supposed, with a respectable force to the frontier of Texas, either by way of San Luis Potoso [sic], or direct to Monte Rey [sic] . . ."[9]

Articles picked up from Mexican newspapers provided a Mexican perspective on the Texas Revolution: "The colonists of Texas have revolted against the Supreme Government, or to speak more correctly, against the nation, which has shown them such generous hospitality, and lavished upon them means by which they might live, and even enrich themselves . . . What those ungrateful men aspire to is, to rob Mexico of the fertile soil to which they were admitted, without any other condition than submission to the laws of the country, which they hypocritically swore to obey . . . The Supreme Government has called into action all its resources, and the Supreme Congress was engaged last night in devising new ones to preserve the Mexican Territory entire, and to make an example of the ungrateful and wicked adventurers, who attempt to dismember it and insult the generous nation which gave them shelter and hospitality.

"We have been assured that an express was sent last night to call the illustrious conqueror of Tampico [i.e., Antonio Lopez de Santa Anna] to come and place himself at the head of the troops that are on their march against these land pirates of a new description. Now, more than ever, we should be wise, and rally round the Supreme Government, to avoid becoming the plaything of a handful of banditti, whom we have inconsiderately favored."[10]

Meanwhile, volunteers from the United States were making their way to Texas:

New York, Nov. 18.
   THE TEXAS VOLUNTEERS.—A vessel will depart to-morrow for Texas, with nearly two hundred Volunteers. She goes direct to New Orleans, which port is to be the rendezvous for four other vessels also with volunteers. Immediately after their arrival they will leave in a body for Texas.[11]

Some of the New York volunteers, perhaps this very group, ran into some difficulties in trying to make their way to New

Orleans. The following letter illustrates the fate of some volunteers who left New York in the vessel *Madawaska*:

NASSAU, (N. P.) Dec. 10, 1835.

Dear Sir:—I write from an English prison yard. You will laugh at this, and indeed I do myself. But so it is. Here I am, in company with my associates in tribulation, for the crime of Piracy! Don't stare now, and I will tell you how it happened. After leaving New York, we had a fair wind for eight or ten days, at the end of which time, we found ourselves among the Bahama banks and islands. Our captain, never having sailed the route before, lost his reckoning, and we were carried into a dangerous and almost unknown harbor. He then sent a boat on shore to an island called Elentheris, with 17 men on board, who, contrary to his wishes, took with them a quantity of arms and ammunition. On the island they found the inhabitants to consist principally of blacks.—Having indulged themselves pretty freely in spirits, and finding the inhabitants rather weak and ignorant, they commenced hostilities upon their effects, such as fowls, pigs, Indian meal, &c. and so terrified the people that they would do whatever they required. They commanded them with drawn pistols at their heads, and threatened them with instant death if they disobeyed. This indiscreet conduct of course occasioned and excited feeling on being known at Nassau, and two gun ships were immediately sent in pursuit of us, with strict orders to board us, and put us all to death if we made the least resistance.—After searching near a week, one of them hailed us about 1 o'clock, P.M., with the salutation "send a boat on board, or we shall fire into you." We of course complied, and they made us their prisoners, conveyed us to this place, and we are now in a prison yard."[12]

While the New York volunteers were whiling away their time in a British prison, the Volunteers already in Texas, and besieging San Antonio de Bexar, attacked the city:

TEXAS AND MEXICO.
From the New Orleans Bee.
GLORIOUS NEWS FROM TEXAS!
'Freedom's battles once begun,
Bequeathed from bleeding sire to son,
Tho' battled oft is surely won.'

St. Antonia [sic], the last fortress of the despot Santana [sic], in Texas, has fallen!!

The valor and perseverance of the colonial troops were irresistible. This ever to be remembered event, took place on Thursday, Dec. 10th. On the Saturday previous (the 5th,) 300 of the Colonial troops entered the town of San Antonio, under the command of Col. Benj. R. Milam. They could not at first get possession of the public square, owing to the walls and ditches across the mouths of the streets, each of which was likewise defended by two pieces of artillery, and in consequence of this, they occupied some buildings and tops of houses adjacent. Here they remained battling unceasing night and day, until Wednesday the 9th inst. when they forced their way into the square and drove the enemy across the river into their fort, called the 'Alamo.'

In these relative situations the battle continued until Thursday 10th, when the enemy capitulated.[13]

Sadly, "the joy of triumph was sadly diminished by the circumstance that the brave Milam, the dauntless leader of the storm, was numbered among the slain. He fell by a ball through his head while fearlessly animating his men to victory. Long! long will Texas and the friends of liberty remember and lament his fate. Among the gallant band who stormed the town were more than 100 volunteers from the U.S. of the north. The New Orleans Greys and Blues constituted a great majority of these, and the remainder were from different parts of the State of Mississippi. The whole of them were among the first and foremost where the battle raged hottest, and displayed throughout, the undaunted bravery of disciplined regulars."[14]

After their successful siege and capture of Bexar, the young Texian army fell apart, with many going home and others marching on an ill-fated expedition to Matamoros. We next hear from the forces left at Bexar in the following:

> LATEST FROM TEXAS.—We received intelligence from Texas, by which we learn that an express had been sent on the 14th ult. from Colonel Neill, commanding at San Antonio, informing the provincial government that a force of 2500 men had been at Lared[o], a short time before, and that 1500 of them had advanced as [far as] the Rio Frio, 80 miles from San

Antonio. An attack on the latter place was daily expected. In the Alamo there were then only 75 men, with little provisions. The Acting Governor had issued a proclamation on the 9th ult. calling on volunteers, to go to the defense of San Antonio.[15]

On 23 February 1836, General Santa Anna arrived with his army and the Texian forces, now under William Barret Travis and James Bowie, retreated into the Alamo. The news did not arrive in New Orleans until 15 March and it was 16 April before newspapers in Ohio received word. They reported that "the town of San Antonio had fallen into the hands of Santa Anna and his army—about 4000 in number. By forced marches, Santa Anna took the citizens by surprise; and they were obliged to fly into the garrison. There were about 200 in the fort, well prepared and furnished with provisions. When Santa Anna sent them orders for an immediate and unconditional surrender, they replied that they must attest their strength; and that they were able to hold out against any army of his, even if it contained 5000 men."[16]

Of course, they were only able to hold out for thirteen days. In the pre-dawn hours of 6 March 1836, Santa Anna stormed the Alamo. This news did not reach Midwestern newspapers until 23 April but the news was electrifying. "Bexar has fallen! Its garison [sic] was only 187 strong, commanded by Lieut. Col. W. Travis. After standing reported attacks for two weeks, and an almost constant cannonade and bombarding during that time, the last attack was made . . . by upwards of two thousand men, under the command of Santa Anna in person; they carried the place about sunrise, with the loss of 520 men killed, and about the same number wounded. After about an hour's fighting the whole garrison was put to death (save the sick and wounded and seven men who asked for quarter).—All fought desperately, until entirely cut down; the rest were coolly murdered. The brave and gallant Travis, to prevent his falling into the hands of the enemy, shot himself. Not an individual escaped . . . Cols. James Bowie and David Crockett are among the slain; the first was murdered in his bed, to which he had been confined by illness—the latter fell, fighting like a tiger."[17]

The majority of U.S. newspapers were shocked by the massacre at the Alamo. However, this was not true of all newspapers. The editors of the *Catholic Telegraph* of Cincinnati, Ohio had their own view on the Battle of the Alamo and on the Texas Revolution in general:

> Is it an unheard of thing, when a fortress has been summonded [sic] and has refused to surrender, and is afterwards carried by storm, that quarter has been refused! And does the putting to death of seven men by an enraged soldiery, under these circumstances, excite so much horror in a country where the good people are in the habit of seizing on gamblers and incendiaries, first torturing them with the whip, and then hanging them up in cold blood?
> . . .
> And what sort of incendiaries were the hon. David Crockett, and the illustrious Jesse Benton; and for what purpose, we should like to know, did they go into Texas?
> . . .
> The sole cause of the war is this. The Mexican constitution prohibits slavery. The Texians want to introduce it. They know that slaves can be imported from Africa for less than a hundred dollars a head; they have some already; they have found them very profitable, and they are anxious for more. Nearly three years ago, Mr. Austin went to Mexico, to obtain the sanction of the government to a constitution, which the colonists had formed, by which slavery was permitted. The Congress refused to consent. Austin then commenced some intrigues towards secession, which were discovered, and he was imprisoned at Mexico. Afterwards, by the favor of Santa Anna, he was released; but he had no sooner returned to Texas, than he set on foot the present rebellion.[18]

Next in the string of disasters to Texian arms occurred to the men of James Walker Fannin's command. This was reported from a private letter picked up from a Mexican newspaper: "This day, Palm Sunday, March [27], has been to me a season of most heart felt sorrow. At six in the morning, the execution of 412 American prisoners was commenced, and continued till eight, when the last of the number was shot. At 11, began the operation of burning the bodies. Who can tell when they will be consumed!!"[19]

The next reports from Texas were of the movements of the Texian army under Sam Houston: "Gen Houston with 2000 men has marched against a division of the Mexicans, 1200 strong, which had crossed the Colorado, and were unable to receive any reinforcement in consequence of the sudden overflowing of that stream, thereby rendering their junction with Santa Anna impracticable."[20]

The final act in the Texas Revolution was the Battle of San Jacinto on 21 April 1836. I found an article on the battle printed exactly one month later, on 21 May: "an express has arrived here, via Natchitoches, from Texas, and is confirmed by Gen. Gain[e]s, that Gen. Houston, of Texas has conquered Santa Anna, and his army.—Santa Anna himself, and his soldiers, all prisoners . . . The saddle of Santa Anna was taken and brought in, and is of a costly order, being estimated as worth between six and eight hundred dollars, and the express who brought in the news, rode on the horse of Santa Anna . . ."

Notes

1. Anonymous, "Postscript," *Western Courier. And Piqua Enquirer*, Piqua, Ohio, 16 April 1836.
2. Anonymous, "Texas," *The Gazette*, Volume V, Number 30, Bellefontaine, Ohio, 10 October 1835.
3. Anonymous, "War in Texas," *The Gazette*, Volume V, Number 37, Bellefontaine, Ohio, 31 October 1835.
4. Anonymous, "Texas," *The Gazette*, Bellefontaine, Ohio, 5 December 1835.
5. *Ibid*.
6. Anonymous, "Latest from Texas," *The Gazette*, Bellefontaine, Ohio, 5 December 1835.
7. Anonymous, "Latest from Texas," *Western Courier and Piqua Enquirer*, Volume 1, Number 42, Piqua, Ohio, 2 January 1836.
8. Anonymous, "Still Later," *The Gazette*, Bellefontaine, Ohio, 5 December 1835.
9. Anonymous, "Late from Mexico," *Toledo Blade*, Number 1, Volume I, Toledo, Ohio, 19 December 1835.
10. *Ibid*.
11. Anonymous, "The Texas Volunteers," *Toledo Blade*, Number 1, Volume I, Toledo, Ohio, 19 December 1835.
12. Anonymous, "Texas Volunteers," *Western Courier, and Piqua Enquirer*, Volume 1, Number 44, Piqua, Ohio, 16 January 1836.

13. Anonymous, "Texas and Mexico," *Western Courier and Piqua Enquirer*, Volume I, Number 46, Piqua, Ohio, 30 January 1836.
14. *Ibid*.
15. Anonymous, "Latest From Texas," Volume I, Number 52, *Western Courier. And Piqua Enquirer*, Piqua, Ohio, 12 March 1836.
16. Anonymous, "Texas," Volume I, Number 41, *Western Aurora. And Farmers and Mechanics' Advocate*, Bellefontaine, Ohio, 16 April 1836.
17. Anonymous, "The fall of Bexar—The entire of the troops in Garrison put to death—Cols. Crocket and Bowie killed!" Volume 6, Number 6, *Bellefontaine Gazette. And Logan County Advertiser*, Bellefontaine, Ohio, 23 April 1836.
18. Anonymous, "Texas and Mexico," Volume V, Number 19, *Catholic Telegraph, Devoted to Religion, Literature, and General Intelligence*. Cincinnati, Ohio, 19 May 1836.
19. Anonymous, "Goliad Massacre," Volume 6, Number 12, *Bellefontaine (Ohio) Gazette. And Logan County Advertiser*, Bellefontaine, Ohio, 4 June 1836).
20. Anonymous, "Mexico," Volume 2, Number 10, *Western Courier And Enquirer*, Piqua, Ohio, 21 May 1836.

A Fortnight with James Bowie

By the Rev. Benjamin Chase
Edited by William C. Davis

It is not often that we get a new glimpse into the pre-Alamo life of James Bowie, though more and more such sources gradually come to light. First-person recollections by those who knew him well are especially scarce, and that alone makes the account of time spent with him in 1833 by Benjamin Chase of great significance for Bowie scholars.

For two weeks Chase and Bowie traveled together, became well acquainted, and remained thereafter friendly for several months. As a result, Chase is able to provide us with a telling look at aspects of Bowie's personality and character for which we have precious little evidence, including his humor, his attitude toward religion, his sense of fair play, even his health and drinking. So much of Bowie's life is limned only by the wide trail of legal documents he left behind—most of them evidence of his extensive land fraud schemes—that it is especially welcome to have something that fills out the human dimensions of a an undoubtedly remarkable man.

Even though internal evidence makes it apparent that "The Autobiography of Reverend Benjamin Chase" was written in 1863, some thirty years after the events he describes, still his recollection was in the main excellent, even in some small details. Internal evidence indicates that Chase may have made notes of his conversations with Bowie even earlier, when the memories were fresh. He reveals much that is new, including Bowie's inter-

"Jim Bowie's San Saba Fight" by Gary Zaboly, Alamo Journal, no. 131 (Dec. 2002).

est in the Texas fur trade, provides a very accurate account of the 1831 fight with Tawakonis, and gives us perhaps our only surviving account of the 1827 Sandbar fight to come—indirectly, to be sure—from Bowie's own lips.

The Rev. Benjamin Chase was born November 20, 1789, in Litchfield, New Hampshire, and graduated from Middlebury College before spending several years teaching school in New Jersey and later New Orleans. Later ordained in Connecticut by the Congregational branch of the Presbyterian Church, he became an agent for the American Bible Society and moved to Mississippi, near Natchez. Chase first visited Texas in 1833, where he engaged Sumner Bacon to act as agent for distributing bibles in the Mexican colony, and it was while on this mission that he encountered Bowie. After his return from his visit, Chase would help establish the Presbyterian Synod of Mississippi in 1834, including Texas in its work, and he became chairman of the Synod's executive committee. Thereafter until his death in 1870 he retained a keen interest in ecclesiastical affairs in Texas, including being an active friend of Austin College.[1]

The excerpt that follows is taken from a typewritten transcript prepared sometime in the twentieth century. The transcript contains numerous inaccuracies in spelling and grammar, while punctuation is especially erratic. It seems far more likely that this is the result of careless transcription by the copyist, than that such commonplace errors escaped correction by the editors of the original publication in the *Southwestern Presbyterian* in the 1890s. The typed transcript states that it appeared in two parts in the *Southwestern Presbyterian*, published at New Orleans. Part I supposedly appeared in the issues dated December 24, 1891, and February 18, 1892; Part II in issues dated October 1 and November 19, 1891. Clearly this makes no sense, as it has Part II appearing earlier than Part I. Considering the apparent carelessness of the transcription elsewhere, it is probable that the transcriber accidentally transposed the dates, and that Part I should have been listed as appearing October 1 and November 19, 1891, and Part II on December 24, 1891 and February 18, 1892. Unfortunately, an extensive search has failed to locate any of these issues of the *Southwestern Presbyterian* that survive, making it impossible to check the dates or the text for accuracy.

This excerpt from the "Autobiography of the Reverend Benjamin Chase" is taken from the original typescript in Volume 183, pages 196-202, of the Francois Mignon Collection at Northwestern State University of Louisiana in Natchitoches, and is published by permission.

Benjamin Chase Narrative of James Bowie, May-November 1833

Early in May 1833, Benjamin Chase arrived in Natchitoches, Louisiana, intending to go into Texas to arrange for the distribution of bibles for his employer the American Bible Society. While there he had a visit from Dr. John Sibley, an influential jurist and friend of Texas, who brought a plea from Sam Houston that Chase give up his plan of going to Texas. Pointing out that it was a Catholic province in which Protestant clergymen were not welcome, Houston warned that Chase risked arrest once he reached Nacogdoches. Undaunted, Chase pressed on, and the very day after leaving Natchitoches he came upon Houston and others at a spring where they were having an impromptu party mixing brandy with the spring's cool water. Houston no doubt repeated the warning, but Chase turned a deaf ear to him. Within a few days he had reached Nacogdoches, concluded arrangements with Sumner Bacon to distribute bibles without molestation, and was on his way to San Antonio. He crossed the San Pedro about May 20, and then reached Robbins' Ferry on the Trinity, having already encountered difficulties on the road due to widespread flooding from spring rains.

As it was still raining, I remained that night with Mr. Robbins, proprietor of the ferry, and proceeded again in the morning, quite uncertain how far I should be able to go.[2] In the early part of the day, I came to an overflowed swamp, in which I had not probably ridden more than a hundred and fifty yards when I saw a number of travellers on mules, swimming toward me, one of whom called and requested me to remain where I was, until he came. On his arrival, he requested me to "take his watch out of his hat and hold it until he returned from releasing one of his mules, entangled in the vines a short distance below, and might cause him to lose it in the water."

On his return, he inquired, "Are you a stranger here?" Entirely so, I replied. "Then I advise you not to go any farther until the water subsides, because between here and the Brazos, the overflow of two swamps is united, and unless you are acquainted, there is only one place in several miles, where your horse could rest by touching bottom; it will therefore be unsafe, and I advise you not to attempt it." Thanking him for his counsel, I accompanied him back to Mr. R's from whence I came in the morning. After our clothing was partially dry, my adviser left the room, for a short time, and the landlord inquired of me, "Are you acquainted with that man?" I am not—never saw him until I met him in the water this morning, but have found him very civil and kind for a stranger. Greatly to my surprise, he informed me, "That was the celebrated desperado, Jim Bowie."

He had with him ten men armed and carrying their provisions for the journey on pack mules. After his marriage with the daughter of the Governor of a Mexican Province, he contracted for the exclusive privilege of carrying on the Fur trade for 14 years, on the head waters of the Brazos and Colorado, and also, for reopening and working the San Saba Silver Mine, in the same region.[3] John Austin, (Stephen's brother) had made a temporary Treaty with about 1500 Indians, who were planting corn near the Waco Village which would interfere with B's plans, and he had started to visit them for the purpose of ascertaining correctly their force, and how armed, that he might prepare to attack and destroy them, about the time their corn would be ripe in the Fall: but finding the country so over-flowed, he had been obliged to change his course, as I had mine, and was on his way to Louisiana.[4]

The next morning we recrossed the Trinity and overflowed prairie, and within a day or two, were joined by three Colonists, and at the San Pedro by Mrs. N. and her Guard, escorting her over the Sabine.[5] She manifested no grief at her banishment, traveled in rear of the company, apparently without fatigue, or mental distress, and seemed to rest as quietly as any of the party, encamped on the ground.

We arrived at Nacogdoches on Saturday morning,[6] and instead of "causing disturbance, and being put in the Calaboose," as General Houston kindly notified me, "I probably should be," the citizens sent a Committee to request me to remain and preach for them on the Sabbath. Bowie was standing near, and immediately remarked to me, "By all means, grant the request, and I will wait for you with my men, until Monday." I agreed to do so.

After taking some refreshments, B. proposed to accompany and introduce me to the Catholic Priest. I gladly availed myself of his politeness and went. On the Padre's entering the room, I was introduced as a Protestant Minister from the United States. He advanced and embraced me in his arms, saying (according to B's interpretation), I am glad to see you here, engaged in the same good cause that I am."

He was a Capuchin Friar, tall for a native Spaniard, quite slender and stooping barefoot, wearing his cowl, clad in a robe of coarse sackcloth, trailing a yard or more, and girded with a very stout cord, or rope of the same material, in which were tow or three large knots—made a short address, which Bowie, without knowing he understood any English, was interpreting freely, and making me too welcome, until he began to correct him. Bowie, apologized, saying, it had been so long since he had much to do with Ecclesiastic matters, he might have made some mistake, which he hoped he would excuse. And if he would be so kind as to repeat what he wished communicated, he would endeavor to be more particular. The Padre repeated, which, in substance, was much as before, that "He had no orders, either from his Government, or from his Bishop, to welcome, or forbid a Protestant coming to the Province, that he had felt very sorry for the Colonists, and wished he could teach then—had once or twice attempted it, through an Interpreter, which was so imperfectly done, he believed it was labor lost, could only say, he was glad to see some one there who could instruct them in a language which they understood."[7]

After our return, B. said he would go and persuade the Padre to attend our service on the Sabbath, but soon came back shaking his head, and saying, "It will not do."

On Sabbath morning May 26th, 1833, I preached in one of the largest houses in Nacogdoches, to about 150 persons, nearly half of whom, were said to be Mexicans, who probably understood little, if anything, that was said—all paying the most respectful attention throughout, although the singing was of rather an extraordinary character. When I announced the Hymn, no one seemed willing, if able, to start the tune. Bowie came forward, took hold of the book with me, and commenced singing something, so much resembling a tune which I had heard, I was able to assist him in striking it, when several others joined in, and we thus praised God in the best melody that we could make. Probably no other Protestant Minister in America, ever had such a chorister to assist in leading the devotions of a Religious Assembly! And however incongruous it may seem, to have declined his aid, when proffered in that manner would doubtless have created serious disturbance, if not wholly interrupted our worship. There were a few Protestant Christians present, who had not heard a sermon for several years—others had never heard one, and eternity can only disclose the good that may have been done by attempting to worship God, even under such untoward circumstances.

NOTE: By Dr. Chase: Bowie subsequently apologized for commencing the tune so awkwardly. Said his mother was a member of the Methodist Church, and when he was small, often had preaching at their house, and he learned several of their tunes. But it had been so long since he tried to sing one, he had nearly forgotten them all.

After the services were concluded, a man told me he lived 18 miles from there, on the road to the Sabine, and requested permission to notify his neighbors that I would preach at his house the next day at 11 A.M. Bowie heard it, and said, "Yes, do so, and I will wait for you." The appointment was made and I fulfilled it in a crowded house of small dimensions, filled with an attentive, and apparently grateful audience—Bowie present.[8]

Lest I should leave too favorable impression of the Padre's good will towards the Protestant Colonists, I ought to state that before I left Nacogdoches on Monday morning, the Alcalde came and told me, "The Padre did send me word on Saturday evening, dar was to be Protestant preaching tomorrow, and it was my business to look into dat. I did not wish to offend de Patre, neder [neither] did I wish to interrupt de Protestant preaching: so I tell my wife to go to de preaching and I take my horse and ride out into de country, and just come in." There seemed to be reason therefore, to fear, that the Padre's embrace was less cordial than he pretended.[9]

On my return, Mr. Bacon had received the Bibles, and was distributing them which afforded the gratification of feeling, that although prevented from going as far into the interior as was intended, yet the main object had been accomplished by providing for the speedy supply of the inhabitants with the Holy Scriptures.[10]

Brought into such company, by the Providence of God, I traveled with Bowie about 15 days, sharing his hospitality and receiving at all times, the most kind and respectful attention. Besides being armed with a rifle and pistols, he had his favorite weapon, the "Bowie Knife" about sixteen inches in length, nearly two in width, and half an inch in thickness, giving it almost the weight of a "Meat Cleaver," and rendering it one of the most formidable instruments that man ever wields against his fellow man. It will perhaps convey some idea of its force, to state "That in wiping his knife after cutting our jerked venison and bear meat in a grove where we had been eating, he gave a Black Jack (tree) about the size of a man's wrist, a little stroke, severing it as though it had been a straw.[11]

He rode constantly by my side and seemed to take pleasure in relating his exploits. Told me of his turning the Alcalde back when going for a file of men to prevent Mr. Bacon from having a Camp Meeting.[12] Said, "he spent a day at his meeting, on his return from Natchitoches—saw he was getting along very well—took a drink of whiskey, wishing him success, and went on his way."[13] Mentioned several of his rencounters with Indians, one of which I had often heard spoken of as characteristic of him. An Indian was angry about something, and made a threat against the "bug Captain" as they called him. Bowie proposed that "they should sit facing each other on a log, and settle it with their knives." The Indian consented, and was almost instantly cut to pieces.[14] He gave me the particulars of his bloody affray at Natchez in September 1827, of which I had a memorandum. A number of persons came over from Alexandria, consisting of two or three parties, to settle their difficulties by duels, on the sandbar in the middle of the river, opposite to the city. Bowie came as second for one of them, and Colonel Crane for another.[15] The first fight was between Doctor Mattox and Mr. Wells—the second between General Cuney and Mr. Wright[16]—"After which," Bowie said, "He[17] told Col. Crane, with whom there had been a misunderstanding for some time, that they might as well settle their difficulty then, as ever—on which "he said," Crane and Blanchard[18] both shot him through the body and he fell—others of the party stabbed him with dirks, and cut him on the head with a sword. While thus prostrate, one of them was about to thrust him again with a sword Cone [cane], and he caught the tail of his coat, pulled him down, and gave him the whole length of his blade.[19] It did my very soul good," said he, to wrench it through his heart, and kill such a mean puppy, who would stab a man already down, and supposed to be dying, as they thought I was, and I was not very far from it either, for besides shooting me twice through the body, and cutting me over the head with a sword, I was stabbed in 14 places: but drinking half a pint of brandy made me feel better, so I was moved away from there "in time to avoid the Magistrate, who was about to arrest me.[20]

NOTE: by Doctor Chase. Colonel Crane who was only wounded in the foot, was brought over to Natchez: but was soon removed also, to avoid the Magistrate.[21]

"Butchered as I was," said he, "it was long before I recovered from the injuries. My scalp continued sore, and in bad condition, and in the healing of the wounds in my body, something adhered internally, which prevented the free use of my limbs, three or four years, until a hard fight with the Indians broke everything loose, and set all right.[22] I was on my way to the San Saba river in 1831, with ten men, one of them an old hunter, [who] told me to put a bear's paunch on my head for a cap, leaving a hole in the top, for pouring in bear's oil every morning, and it would soon be well.[23] It was several days before we saw a bear, and in the meantime, I tried a deer's paunch, which became stiff and injured my head. At length, killing a fat bear, I converted his maw into a cap, pouring in bear's oil every morning, I suppose somewhat as Aaron was annointed, and in a short time, my head was well, and troubled me no more.

When within two days easy travel of San Saba, a runner came from Isaonie, the Comanche Chief, to inform me that 164

Indians (124 Wacos and Tawackanies, and 40 Caddos) were on our trail, and would probably attack us the next day: and in proof of his being such a messenger, shewed the well known Voucher, the Chief's Silver Medal.[24] I at first thought of trying to reach the old Fort at San Saba, but concluded a forced march, through the night, would unfit us for visiting so numerous a foe, and therefore halted near a stream early in the evening, and made such preparation for our defence as we could consistently with our taking needful rest.[25]

The next morning the Indians were in full view, and at an early hour, headed by their Chief, whooping and cheering them on, they made a vigorous attack.[26] We awaited their fire in silence, and had one of our men crippled in the leg.[27] A ball from our rifles broke the Chief's thigh and killed his horse. Another took his place and soon shared a similar fate.[28] We took care to make every shot with our rifles tell, which soon diministed [sic] their number, and they attempted to occupy a rising ground partly in our rear, but were so promptly met, it was soon abandoned, having previously wounded another of our men, whom we placed behind our defence, and was able to assist in loading our guns.

They next got within the banks of the stream in our rear, where one of our wounded men kept his eye ranging, and shot every head that peeped above the ground, which drove them from that position.[29] They next went to the wind ward and fired the grass, intending to route us by that means: but our wounded men burnt away the grass around, which prevented the flames from reaching them and thus defeated that design. The contest lasted through the day, until darkness compelled it to cease: but we expected to renew it in the morning and probably continue it while there was a man left. But when the day dawned, there was not an Indian in sight—bloody places on the matted grass, indicated where their dead and wounded had lain, which we afterward learned from the Comanches amounted to 83—our loss one killed and three wounded.[30] We remained there eight days, recruiting our strength, and then, with five horses killed, and three badly wounded, were obliged to carry two of our wounded men on litters, and on the twelfth day arrived at San Antonio. The fight, said Bowie, "together with carrying the men, broke everything loose that adhered in my side, and I have been a perfectly well man ever since."[31]

I thought it quite probable a liberal allowance ought to be made on this representation of the combat: but incidentally meeting with the *Philadelphia Evening Post* before I reached home, my attention was attracted by the picture of an Indian scene which I found to be Bowie's San Saba fight. His brother, Razin P. Bowie, who was one of the party, being then under treatment by a Occulist in Philadelphia, had furnished the above paper with the account, substantially agreeing with his brother's to me, in the main facts, and differing only in the more minute detail of particulars—thus showing how desperate such a prolonged contest must have been, between parties, whose numerical strength differed more than sixteen to one![32]

Spain commenced her settlements in Texas, by establishing "Missions" as early as 1692, connecting a Cathedral with a Fort in each Presidio. The priests were required to instruct the people, so that they could read their prayers, and I do not recollect meeting one, who could not do that. Those old structures were usually of stone, as at San Antonio, Goliad, Bastrop, San Saba, etc., but the Cathedral at Nacogdoches, was of earth, and the walls perforated for small arms, which were found useful in the contest with the Colonists, two years before I was there.

Their "Mission" was established at San Saba in 1725, where they successfully worked a silver mine for some time, but the Indians feared some evil was intended by the Fort, and watching an opportunity when the gates were open, rushed in and destroyed the whole party, and nearly demolished the Fort.[33] It had remained in that condition about one hundred years, when Bowie started to visit it, and was attacked by the Wacos and Tawacanies, as above stated. It was partly to be revenged on them, as well as to prepare for his future operations, that he had started to visit them, when I met him in the water, directing his way to Louisiana.

When we arrived at Natchitoches, the cholera was prevailing, and great consternation among the people, although not many deaths had occurred—were detained there three days, before the arrival of a boat, on which we could leave—during that time, Bowie and his party, indulged in a most boisterous carousal, pretending "they were trying to keep off the Cholera."[34]

Finding the Colonists who had been our traveling companions, several days, were offering all three of their animals for fifty five dollars, I purchased them. One was a dark chestnut bay poney, of beautiful form, from the mountainous region of Mont Clova[35], remarkably active, gentle, and sure-footed, whose pace was almost like the gliding of a serpent over the earth, without perceptible jar. I presented him to my aged father-in-law believing he would be able to enjoy healthful morning rides, with the least possible degree of fatigue. But how great was our disappointment in finding his first ride terminate within one rod of the house, where he stopped perfectly still, and neither persuasion nor punishment could induce him to move, except beside another horse! The other two animals proved valuable, one serving me upwards of thirty years, until taken away by the Yankee soldiers during the War.

Our boat touched Alexandria, where Bowie had an opportunity to enjoy a dirk and pistol fight, as an amateur. Soon after the landing of the boat, a man came running on board, with the blood flowing freely from his breast, and concealed himself behind a door near which I was sitting—presently, another hastily entered the cabin, with a pistol in one hand, raw hide whip in the other, and was not long in finding the object of his pursuit. The Officers pitched them both headlong from the boat, and there they furiously attacked each other with their weapons. Bowie immediately interfered, seizing hold of them both and saying, "This is not the way to fight"—placed them a few feet apart, fixed their weapons, and said "Now try it, and I'll see fairplay." They fearfully wounded each other, but neither was dead when the boat left, and I heard nothing further respecting them.[36]

Although there was some Cholera on our boat, I escaped sickness, but was not wholly proof against the fatigue and exposure of such a journey.[37] Obliged to swim streams and frequently lie in my wet clothes then and on former occasions, both in summer and winter, began to shew that nature must yield when "Pressed out of measure, above strength," and my right arm became completely paralysed and useless, nearly three months.

The same exposure affected my horses limbs much in the same way, causing him to stumble and pitch headlong, incapable of rising rubbed hard for considerable time, and then perhaps not go more than a hundred and fifty, or two hundred yards, before he would fall again in the same way. Conveying him home by boat, and keeping him warmly covered, daily rubbing his limbs, and giving him gentle exercise, he so far recovered in a few months, as to be able to carry me abroad again, dispensing the Word of Life.

Soon after Bowie's arrival from Alexandria, he visited his mother at Plaquimin, where he had a severe attack of bilious fever, and as soon as sufficiently recovered, returned to Natchez just as the Yellow Fever began to attract attention, and was soon prostrated by that.[38] About the fifth day of his illness, I received intelligence that he was not expected to survive, and went to see him. Found him very ill but conscious, thanked me for calling, "Did not know but what he should make a die of it that time; but rather thought he should weather it." His language was soon incoherent and restlessness so great, my stay was brief, and I thought it quite probable our next interview would be in eternity with his day of probation ended, and oh what a prospect for such a being![39] But in less than three weeks he called upon me at Mantua, said he came to thank me for visiting him when sick, rested an hour or two, took some refreshment and returned to Natchez the same day.

I next heard of him in October, at a Methodist Camp Meeting near Whitestown, below Woodville.[40] A man from New Orleans was boisterously denouncing some one to a listening crowd, when Bowie advanced near and inquired, "Sir, of whom are you speaking?" He replied, "I am speaking of Chase at Second Creek, who collected the Certificates which aided Presbytery in deposing the Rev. Theodore Clapp from the Ministry." "Do you know Mr. Chase?" inquired Bowie. "No, and never wish to." "I do know him," said he, "and let me hear you mention his name again disrespectfully, if you dare—my name is Jim Bowie." That ended the matter, said my informant (Maj. J. L. T.), "he uttered not another word."

A short time after, when about leaving the vicinity of Alexandria to return to Texas, a mule plunged headlong with him down a precipitous Bayou and broke some of his ribs which delayed his departure several days.[41] But little more was known of his career, except that it ended by the Mexicans butchering him in the Alamo, while sick in bed, having first slain a number of his assailants before they could dispatch him.[42]

Notes

1. Jessie Guy Smith, Heroes of the Saddle Bags: *A History of Christian Denominations in the Republic of Texas* (San Antonio, 1951), pp. 109, 119, 133.
2. Nathaniel Robbins operated a ferry over the Trinity Rover on the Old San Antonio Road near today's crossing of State Highway 21.
3. Bowie married Maria Ursula Veramendi, the daughter of Juan Martín de Veramendi, lieutenant governor of Coahuila y Texas, on April 25, 1831. This is the first known mention of Bowie's interest in promoting a fur trade in Texas. Foxes, otter, and other furbearing animals were then plentiful in eastern and central Texas.
4. Located where the city of Waco stands today, the Waco Village was ancient even then. In about 1830 Cherokees had driven the Wacos out, though there were no more than a few hundred of them rather than the 1,500 Chase recalls. John Austin was not Stephen Austin's brother, but his cousin, and in any case Chase is probably referring to Austin's brother James E. B. Austin.
5. Mrs. N. is unidentified. San Pedro Creek is in Houston County.
6. May 25, 1833.
7. Catholicism was the official religion of Mexico, including Texas, and Protestant worship was forbidden by law, but Mexican authorities rarely ever attempted to enforce the statute.
8. This would have been in the neighborhood of current Garrison.
9. At this time the alcalde would have been José Ignacio Ibarvo.
10. Sumner Bacon came to Texas in 1829 as a Presbyterian missionary, and early in 1833 Chase had recommended him as agent in Texas for the American Bible Society to distribute Protestant testaments to the colonists.
11. Chase's description of Bowie's knife certainly differs from earlier accounts of the blade that was used in the Sandbar fight, especially in its supposed half-inch thickness. Rezin Bowie made that knife and his own description of it is one-and-one-half inches wide and about nine inches long, with no note of its thickness. Of course, after nearly six years, James Bowie may have been carrying a different knife altogether. Just as likely, after thirty years Chase's memory had probably become imprecise and clouded by legendary tall tales about the knife, exaggerating its size.
12. Probably Ibarvo.
13. There are numerous accounts of Bowie preventing a Protestant camp meeting from being broken up by rowdies or Mexican authorities. Chase's

1863 account here is the earliest yet, and is quite possibly the progenitor of them all. The John S. Ford Memoirs, Volume II, p. 332, at the Center for American History, University of Texas at Austin, also contains an account of Bowie assisting a camp meeting being held by Bacon at Nacogdoches. See William C. Davis, *Three Roads to the Alamo: The Lives and Fortunes of James Bowie, David Crockett, and William Barret Travis* (New York, 1998), pp. 666-67n.

14. The knife fight on a log was a common frontier tall tale, though that is not to say that it may not have happened. There are at least three other accounts of Bowie fighting such duels, though with Spaniards or Mexicans rather than an Indian, the earliest dating from 1888. What is significant is that Chase's 1863 account is the earliest found to date, and he states that he had it from Bowie's mouth. Of course, after the passage of thirty years, Chase may be confusing what Bowie told him in 1833 with other stories he had heard since. Then, too, Bowie may have been simply spinning a tall tale for his own amusement, for his brother Rezin stated categorically in 1838 that James Bowie never had a duel of any sort other than the Sandbar fight. See Davis, *Three Roads*, pp. 745n, 749n.

15. Robert Crain.

16. Dr. Thomas Maddox, Samuel Wells, Samuel Cuny, and Norris Wright.

17. Bowie here refers to Cuny, who proposed to Crain that they settle their differences, setting off the Sandbar fight. For a thorough account see James Batson, *James Bowie and the Sandbar Fight: Birth of the James Bowie Legend & Bowie Knife* (Madison, Ala., 1992).

18. Alfred Blanchard.

19. Bowie stabbed Norris Wright

20. An examination of Bowie immediately after the fight revealed a bullet through his lung and another through the thigh, at least seven stabbing wounds, and a gash on his head, not from a sword, but from a pistol thrown at him by Crain. In the confusion he could easily have thought it came from a sword. He was taken across the Mississippi River to Vidalia, Louisiana.

21. Either Bowie misspoke, or else Chase's memory is hazy, for Crane was not reported as injured. Alfred Blanchard was cut by Bowie's knife, and it may have been he who is referred to, though Crain did go to Vidalia after the fight.

22. This account by Bowie, second hand though it may be, is significant evidence of the internal injuries he suffered, and which may have influenced his future health, lending weight to speculations that his final illness in 1836 may have been at least in part pulmonary.

23. It is evident from the account that by "paunch," Chase means the stomach of the animal. This novel "cure" may be nothing more than a frontier tall tale.

24. Bowie and a party of ten others, including his brother Rezin Bowie, left San Antonio on November 2, 1821, on the expedition to the San Saba silver mines. Chase's recollection of Bowie's account is very accurate. While it must be considered possible that he refreshed his memory by reference to Rezin's published account, still Chase adds details not available in print. The messenger from Chief Isayune reached Bowie on November 20, warning of a total of 124 Tawakoni, Waco, and Caddo intending to attack the next day.

25. Bowie's account suggests that he was in overall command of the expedition, as he probably was, though his brother Rezin's later published account seemed to suggest that it was he, the elder brother, who was in charge.

26. November 21, 1831.

27. David Buchanan suffered a broken leg in the first Indian volley.

28. Caiaphas Ham shot down the chief, and Bowie himself shot the mounted leader who replaced him.

29. Matthew Doyle was the wounded man referred to.

30. The Bowies at the time estimated Indian losses as forty killed and thirty wounded. The defenders lost Buchanan, Doyle, and James Coryell wounded, and Thomas McCaslan killed.

31. Chase's account of Bowie's telling of the San Saba fight story is remarkably accurate, even to the number of horses killed.

32. Rezin Bowie's "An Indian Battle," appeared in the Philadelphia *Atkinson's Saturday Evening Post and Bulletin*, August 17, 1833, illustrated by a crude woodcut of the battle to which Chase refers.

33. In fact, the San Saba mission was established in 1757 and on March 16, 1758 the small company of priests and workers were attacked and killed.

34. This will be early in June 1833. Chase's account of Bowie's "carousal" is one of numerous recollections of Bowie's fondness for drink and celebration, though if Bowie were alcoholic at this point in his life, as is sometimes suggested, Chase likely would have spurned his company.

35. Monclova in Coahuila, Mexico.

36. Chase's is the only surviving account of the Louisiana leg of Bowie's 1833 trip from Nacogdoches eastward, on his way to Natchez, New Orleans, and eventually to Philadelphia and New York with his brother Rezin. The account of Bowie's intercession in the brawl in Alexandria also lends weight to his presumed sense of rough-and-tumble "fun."

37. Chase's reference to cholera is ominous, for the epidemic was widespread, and would soon break out in Texas. In September Bowie's wife Ursula would be one of its victims.

38. In 1832 Rezin Bowie lost the family plantation on Bayou Lafourche due to insolvency, and relocated in Iberville Parish, Louisiana, to a small plantation just south of Plaquemine. The Bowies' mother Elve had lived for many years near Opelousas, but must have relocated to live with Rezin's family. After this visit James made his trip to Philadelphia and New York with Rezin. It was on his return from that journey in September that he contracted malaria. The "bilious fever" that Chase mentions may have been anything, given the loose medical definitions of the day, including a manifestation of the probable pulmonary problems that later led to references to his affliction of the lungs.

39. Bowie's malaria came in October 1833 and on the last day of the month, expecting to die, he made out his will.

40 Chase's memory is off here, for in October Bowie was ill with malaria. Since Bowie appears to have stayed some time in Natchez and vicinity recuperating, this episode may have taken place anytime from November 1833 to February 1834, after which time Bowie was back in San Antonio.

41. This accident, previously unknown, is another to add to the catalog of

Bowie's physical illnesses and mishaps, all of which help to illuminate the stories of his drinking from 1834 onward, perhaps in part due to pain, and also lends further weight to the argument that he was suffering chronic internal injuries by 1836, all of them contributing to his apparently severe—and possibly even fatal—illness prior to March 6, 1836.

42. This, of course, is the standard hearsay account of Bowie's death by 1863.

ABOUT THE ARTICLE'S AUTHOR

William C. Davis

William C. Davis is one the nation's most prolific historians. He has authored or edited more than forty books, including such Civil War titles as *Jefferson Davis: The Man and His Hour, Look Away! A History of the Confederate States of America, The Battle of New Market, The Orphan Brigade, The Image of War, The Imperiled Union,* and *Civil War Journal: The Leaders, The Union that Shaped the Confederacy: Robert Toombs and Alexander H. Stephens,* and *An Honorable Defeat: The Last Days of the Confederate Government,* among others.

He was twice nominated for the Pulitzer Prize in History and is the only three-time winner for the Jefferson Davis Award presented for book-length works on Confederate history.

Davis has served as an editor of *American History Illustrated* and *Civil War Times Illustrated.* He was also the on-camera consultant for 52 episodes of the Arts and Entertainment Network/History Channel series *Civil War Journal.*

Although he is best known for his Civil War titles, two of his most important volumes were *Three Roads to the Alamo: The Lives and Fortunes of David Crockett, James Bowie, and William Barret Travis,* and *Lone Star Rising: The Revolutionary Birth of the Texas Republic.*

He wrote "A Fortnight with James Bowie By the Rev. Benjamin Chase," which appeared in issue no. 126 (2002) of *The Alamo Journal.*

William C. Davis is currently Professor of History and Director of Programs at Virginia Tech's Center for Civil War Studies.

Select Bibliography

Abbott, John S. C. *David Crockett: His Life and Adventures*. New York: Dodd, Mead, 1874.

Allen, Charles Fletcher. *David Crockett, Scout, Small Boy, Pilgrim, Mountaineer, Soldier, Bear-Hunter, and Congressman, Defender of the Alamo*. Philadelphia: J. B. Lippincott, 1911.

Barr, Alwyn. *Texans in Revolt: The Battle for San Antonio, 1835*. Austin: University of Texas Press, 1991.

Baugh, Virgil E. *Rendezvous at the Alamo: Highlights in the Lives of Bowie, Crockett, & Travis*. New York: Pageant Press, 1960.

Becerra, Francisco. *A Mexican Sergeant's Recollections of the Alamo and San Jacinto*. Austin: Jenkins Publishing Company, 1980.

Borroel, Roger. *The Papers of Colonel José Enrique de la Peña, Selected Appendixes from his Diary, 1836-1839*. East Chicago, IN: La Villita Publications, 1997.

Burke, James Wakefield. *David Crockett: The Man Behind the Myth*. Austin, Texas: Eakin Press, 1984.

Casteñeda, Carlos Eduardo. *The Mexican Side of the Texas Revolution by the Chief Mexican Participants*. Austin: Graphic Ideas Inc., 1970.

Chariton, Wallace O. *Exploring the Alamo Legends*. Plano, TX: Wordware Publishing, Inc., 1990.

———. *100 Days in Texas: The Alamo Letters*. Plano, TX: Wordware Publishing, Inc., 1990.

Chemerka, William R. *The Alamo Almanac & Book of Lists*. Austin: Eakin Press, 1997.

———. *The Davy Crockett Almanac & Book of Lists*. Austin: Eakin Press, 2000.

Crockett, David. *A Narrative of the Life of David Crockett of the State of Tennessee*. Philadelphia: Carey & Hart, 1834.

Crisp, James E. *Sleuthing the Alamo: Davy Crockett's Last Stand and Other Mysteries of the Texas Revolution*. New York: Oxford Press, 2005.

Daughters of the Republic of Texas. *Muster Rolls of the Texas Revolution*. Austin, 1986.

Davis, William C. *Lone Star Rising: The Revolutionary Birth of the Texas Republic*. New York: Free Press, 2004.

———. *Three Roads to the Alamo: The Lives and Fortunes of David Crockett, James Bowie, and William Barret Travis*. New York: HarperCollins, 1998.

DeShields, James T. *Tall Men with Long Rifles: The Glamorous Story of the Texas

Revolution As Told by Captain Creed Taylor. San Antonio: Naylor Printing Company, 1935.
Edmondson, J. R. *The Alamo Story: From Early History to Current Conflicts*. Plano, Texas: Republic of Texas Press, 2000.
Eggleston, George Cary. *David Crockett*. New York: Dodd, Mead Company, 1875.
Ellis, Edward S. *The Life of Colonel David Crockett*. Philadelphia: Porter & Coates, 1884.
Fehrenbach, T. R. *Lone Star: A History of Texas and Texans*. New York: American Legacy Press, 1983.
Filisola, General Vicente. *The History of the War in Texas*. Translated by Wallace Woolsey. 2 vols. Austin: Eakin Press, 1987.
Foreman, Gary L. *Crockett: The Gentleman from the Cane: A Comprehensive View of the Folkhero Americans Thought They Knew*. Dallas, Texas: Taylor Publishing Company, 1986.
Gaddy, Jerry J. *Texas in Revolt: Contemporary Newspaper Accounts of the Texas Revolution*. Fort Collins, CO: Old Army Press, 1983.
Garland, Hamlin, ed. *The Autobiography of David Crockett*. New York: Charles Scribner's Sons, 1923.
Gray, William F. *From Virginia to Texas, 1835*. Houston: The Fletcher Young Publishing Company, 1965.
Groneman, Bill. *Alamo Defenders: A Genealogy, The People and their Words*. Plano, Texas: Republic of Texas Press, 1990.
_____. *Death of a Legend*. Plano, Texas: Republic of Texas Press, 1999.
_____. *Defense of a Legend: Crockett and the de la Peña Diary*. Plano, Texas: Republic of Texas Press, 1994.
_____. *Eyewitness to the Alamo*. Plano, Texas: Republic of Texas Press, 2001.
Hansen, Todd, ed. *The Alamo Reader: A Study in History*. Mechanicsburg, PA: Stackpole Books, 2003.
Hardin, Stephen L. *Texian Iliad: A Military History of the Texas Revolution*. Austin: University of Texas Press, 1994.
Hauck, Richard Boyd. *Crockett: A Bio-Bibliography*. Westport, Conn.: Greenwood Press, 1982.
Haythornthwaite, Phillip. *The Alamo and the War of Texan Independence*. London: Osprey, 1986.
Jackson, Ron. *Alamo Legacy: Alamo Descendants Remember the Alamo*. Austin: Eakin Press, 1997.
Jenkins, John H., ed. *The Papers of the Texas Revolution, 1835-1836*. 10 vols. Austin: Presidial Press, 1973.
Kilgore, Dan. *How Did Davy Die?* College Station: Texas A&M University Press, 1978.
Lack, Paul D. *The Texas Revolutionary Experience: A Political and Social History, 1835-1836*. College Station: Texas A&M University Press, 1992.
Lofaro, Michael A. *Davy Crockett: The Man, The Legend, The Legacy, 1786-1986*. Knoxville, University of Tennessee Press, 1985.
Lofaro, Michael A., and Joe Cummings, eds. *Crockett at Two Hundred: New Perspectives on the Man and the Myth*. Knoxville, University of Tennessee Press, 1989.

Lord, Walter. *A Time to Stand*. New York: Harper & Brothers, 1961.
McDonald, Archie P. *William Barret Travis: A Biography*. Austin: Eakin Press, 1995.
Mayer, Edwin Justus. *Sunrise in My Pocket, Or The Last Days of Davy Crockett: An American Saga*. New York: Julian Messner, 1941.
Meine, Franklin J., ed. *The Crockett Almanacks: Nashville Series, 1835-1838*. Chicago: The Caxton Club, 1955.
Myers, John Myers. *The Alamo*. New York: E. P. Dutton and Company, 1948.
Nelson, George. *The Alamo: An Illustrated History*. Dry Frio Canyon, TX: Aldine Press, 1998.
Nofi, Albert A. *The Alamo and the War for Texas Independence, September 30, 1835-April 21, 1836*. Conshohocken, PA: Combined Books, Inc., 1992.
Perry, Carmen, ed and trans. *With Santa Anna in Texas: A Personal Narrative of the Revolution by José Enrique de la Peña*. College Station: Texas A&M University Press, 1975.
Potter, Reuben M. *The Fall of the Alamo: A Reminiscence of the Revolution in Texas*. Edited by Charles Grosvenor. Hillsdale, NJ: Otterden Press, 1977.
Procter, Ben H. *The Battle of the Alamo*. Austin: Texas State Historical Association, 1986.
Ragsdale, Crystal Sasse. *The Women and Children of the Alamo*. Austin: State House Press, 1994.
Rosenthal, Phil and Bill Groneman. *Roll Call at the Alamo*. Fort Collins, CO; Old Army Press, 1985.
Rourke, Constance. *Davy Crockett*. New York: Harcourt, 1934.
Santos, Richard G. *Santa Anna's Campaign Against Texas, 1835-1836*. Salisbury, NC: Documentary Publications, 1968.
Schoelwer, Susan Prendergast, with Tom W. Glaser. *Alamo Images: Changing Perceptions of a Texas Experience*. Dallas: DeGolyer Library and Southern Methodist University Press, 1985.
Shackford, James Atkins. *David Crockett: The Man and the Legend*. Chapel Hill: University of North Carolina Press, 1956.
Sprague, William C. *Davy Crockett*. New York: The Macmillan Company, 1915.
Sutherland, John. *The Fall of the Alamo*. San Antonio: Naylor Press, 1936.
Thompson, Frank. *The Alamo: A Cultural History*. Dallas: Taylor Publishing, 2001.
Tinkle, Lon. *13 Days to Glory*. New York: McGraw Hill Book Company, Inc., 1958.
Todish, Tim J. and Terry. *Alamo Sourcebook 1836: A Comprehensive Guide to the Alamo and the Texas Revolution*. Austin: Eakin Press, 1998.
Walraven, Bill and Majorie. *The Magnificent Barbarians: Little Told Tales of the Texas Revolution*. Austin: Eakin Press, 1993.

About the Author

William R. Chemerka is the founder of The Alamo Society, and editor of its quarterly publication, *The Alamo Journal*.

He is the author of *The Alamo Almanac and Book of Lists* (Eakin Press, 1997) and *The Davy Crockett Almanac and Book of Lists* (Eakin Press, 2000). Chemerka is the editor of *The Crockett Chronicle*, a quarterly dedicated to the life and legend of David Crockett. He is also contributing editor at *New Jersey Heritage Magazine*, and has written for *The Star-Ledger*.

Chemerka has appeared as a historical commentator on The History Channel, the Arts and Entertainment Network, C-SPAN Book TV and WCCO (CBS) radio. He was a writer for The History Channel's *First Invasion: The War of 1812*, and served as the featured historian on the Biography Channel's 2002 live webcast, *Live From Austin: The Story of Davy Crockett*.

In 2004, *Texas Monthly* dubbed Chemerka "the Google of Alamo buffs."

Chemerka is a multi-award-winning educator, and is recognized by "Who's Who Among American Teachers." He teaches at The Humanities Center in Peapack-Gladstone, New Jersey, and is a speaker for Americana Lectures.

Chemerka is a member of the Texas State Historical Association, the Company of Military Historians, the Brigade of the American Revolution, the New Jersey Historical Society, the Screen Actors Guild, and the Actor's Equity Association.

www.ingramcontent.com/pod-product-compliance
Lightning Source LLC
Chambersburg PA
CBHW070802100426
42742CB00012B/2224